"Determined to Live is a touching story. Truly inspiring."
— PATRICIA BELL for Reader's favorite

"Richard Ballo has written a story that will bring tears to the eyes of readers and move their hearts in ways they couldn't imagine."
— DIVINE ZAPE for Reader's Favorite

"Kept me glued to the pages,"
— TIM NORTON, Operations Director at SWFL Way-FM

"What will stay most with readers…(is) the incredible spirit and courage Janice showed for the several decades following that fateful night Ron accidentally shot her."
— VIGA BOLAND for Readers' Favorite

Determined
to Live

Determined
to Live

How I survived being shot, paralyzed,
and abandoned by my husband.

As told to and written by
AWARD WINNING AUTHOR

Richard Ballo

Determined to Live
How I survived abusive relationships and raised my kids

Printed in the United States

Published by Tolman Main Press
2670 Horseshoe Dr. N. Suite 203
Naples, FL 34104
1-239-263-0214
www.tolmanmainpress.com

Name: Ballo, Richard
Title: Determined to Live by Richard Ballo
Other Titles: Determined to Live
Description: Naples, FL : Tolman Main Press, [2022]
"A true story of love, violence and the spirit to live."

Library of Congress Control Number: 2022936177
ISBN 978-1-945518-08-9
ISBN 978-1-945518-12-6 (ebook)

Subjects: LCSH: Riddle, Janice | Paralytics—Biography Paralytics—
Psychology | Paralytics—Family relationships | Family violence |
Mothers—Psychology | LCGFT: Autobiographies

Classification: LCC RC406.P3 B35 2017 (print)
LCC RC406.P3 (ebook) | DDC 362.4/3092—dc23

Editorial services: Jill H. Lawrence, Ruby Slippers, Inc. and
www.1106design.com

Cover design: Christine Dupre
Interior design: Jessica Angerstein

CONTENTS

ACKNOWLEDGMENTS

I would like to thank Janice Riddle for her time, confidence, and access into her life during the many phone calls and the visit I made to see her. Getting to know her gave my life perspective. She was truly open about her life and a delight to work with. I would also like to thank her children: Kim, Kari, and Paul, for their time and sharing of their mother's life and encouragement to get their mother's story out. Also thanks to the medical professionals who lent their advice and comments in the writing of this book.

PROLOGUE

In my home town of Naples, Florida, a colleague of mine told me of a woman who had been shot and paralyzed, and was now living with her sister, Pam Moore, at the Marine Corps Base Camp Pendleton in California. The more she told me, the more interested in her story I became. I started phoning Janice and talked with her for several months before I decided to travel to Camp Pendleton to meet the subject of this story in person. I stopped at the guard station at Camp Pendleton and showed the guard my Florida driver's license. I answered a few questions and was allowed to drive onto the base. After a couple of turns I stopped in front of a two-story desert-colored house on a cul-de-sac. I rang the bell. The door was opened by Gunnery Sergeant Pam Moore.

"Her room is there," she said, pointing to the door on the left of the short hallway. Ahead were stairs to the second floor bedrooms. To the right was a door to the laundry room and garage. I had come here to meet Janice Riddle. I was intrigued by her story, and I wanted to meet her. I wanted to know her world.

My knock on her door was acknowledged. The door opened into a short hallway. To the right was a double-door closet. The left wall was covered with family photos: they showed a young, red-headed woman smiling at the camera with her four kids, the oldest child she had when she was just sixteen. She was smiling in every picture. On the far wall were a television and oriental wall hangings. I became aware of a slight hissing sound. Rounding the corner to my right, I saw a large Clinitron bed, a hospital bed that supports an air-circulating system for an inflatable mattress made specifically for paralyzed individuals.

In the bed lay Janice Riddle. Her long red hair was pulled back. She looked small in the bed. Her smile came easily. We grasped hands as we had been phone friends for months.

I pulled up a chair to sit, listen, and learn.

I lived in the house for one week. I observed her living area, mobility, eating habits, speech patterns, and listened to her life story. We left the house twice. One outing consisted of a drive to visit her son Paul and his family, and the other outing was to dinner at the Oceanside Pier in Oceanside, California. Each time I transferred her from her bed to the wheelchair so we could go out. Then after we came back, I transferred her back to her bed.

After visiting Janice, I drove to Garden Grove, California and visited the neighborhood where Janice had lived and the hospital where she was taken after being shot.

I flew back to Naples to be with my young boys. I was no stranger to tragedy as my wife had died of cancer only three years before.

Janice and I resumed our monthly phone calls. I wanted to feel and see the towns and places that Janice described. I wanted to bring her story to life and to do that I needed to not only visit with her but to drive on the streets that she did, to see the trees as she saw. The next year the boys and I flew to Oregon to visit an old friend of mine, see some sights and to visit Scotts Mills, Marquam, and Silverton - the towns where Janice lived.

The story that follows is told through Janice's point of view: her voice, eyes, words, diction, experience and personality, because she's the best at telling her story. Some dramatization is included from information that Janice supplied.

Not all information has been independently verified.

I believe that Janice's life proves that no matter what happens to us, it is how we view the world and respond that shapes how we live. Much time has passed since this book was started. I hope the conditions on healthcare that Janice lived through have changed.

Richard Ballo, 2022

CHAPTER 1

My Mistake

It's Friday night April 17th, 1975 to be exact in Garden Grove, California and I needed a beer.

I am supposed to be on the wagon. I've done real good too about staying clean and sober but a couple of months ago, Ron, he's my second husband and the father of my fourth child - moved out and I started to drink again. At thirty-two years of age, drinking wasn't the only mistake in my life but it's the one that led me here tonight so I could meet Ron and talk things over.

The mistake I needed to talk to Ron about was the mistake I made with Glenn. When Ron moved out I wanted a drinking buddy. That drinking buddy was Ron's workmate, Glenn.

Man was that a big mistake.

I just wanted a drinking buddy to drown my sorrows about Ron leaving me and Glenn was right there, willing and able to take me drinking, take me to dinner, and take down the mileage on my car.

Yes, Glenn was trying to control my life and I would have none of that control stuff. That would have been reliving the worst part of my first marriage and I wasn't going to do that. Also, Glenn had a violent temper just like my first husband, Wayne. Wayne had hit me, but Glenn hadn't.

Besides, I was still married to Ron and still in love with Ron. I was attempting to avoid Glenn and doing a good job at it. Then one night I was at my favorite bar, and I'd had a couple of drinks and was feeling no pain when in walked Glenn. I really didn't want to see him; I just wanted Ron back.

Well, Glenn started drinking too, and then he went to the bathroom. This older guy came over and started talking to me. He wasn't trying to pick me up or anything but when Glenn came back he started yelling at the old guy. And then Glenn hit him. To be real honest, he didn't just hit the poor guy; Glenn punched him until he fell, and then kicked him too. I didn't want to be with a guy with a violent, jealous temper or on the receiving end of it either.

"Get out of my life," I yelled at Glenn, standing as tall as my petite five foot, six-inch frame would allow.

He became quiet.

"If that's what you want, but I want my things I have at your house," he said.

"Get everything," I told him gladly. "Just gather it all up and I'll take you and your things home."

I was right proud of myself. I had spoken up and he was getting out of my life. I drove him to my house in the big Lincoln he had convinced me to buy, and we boxed up his stuff. Then I drove him to his parents' house.

His dad came out and helped carry the boxes from the trunk into the house. His dad carried the last box in, leaving Glenn standing by the driver's door of the car. I started to get in as he was saying something about us, but I wasn't listening because I was putting the key into the ignition.

Suddenly, it felt like a crane was pulling at the top of my head. I realized Glenn was pulling me, all one hundred and twenty pounds of me, out of the car by my hair. Before I could open my mouth to scream, I saw his right hand, with that big old school ring of his, come flying toward me. The blow felt like a Mack truck had run into me.

I was knocked back against the car, seeing stars. Blow after vicious blow struck my face. I don't know where my mind went or how I stood up. After a time my body collapsed to the ground. I still felt the blows come, but now the big steel-toed truckers' boots were flying into my rib cage, making my body jump.

There was no pain, just the thought that "Wow, this is really happening to me."

I don't know how long I was down, but suddenly I found myself in the car, behind the wheel, speeding backwards. I didn't even have the door closed but I got out of there. I believe my guardian angel was driving. My guardian angel has saved me from many things and I praise the Lord for His protection.

The next thing I knew, I was stopped at a red light. I heard someone screaming. I turned to my left and saw a lady in the car next to me screaming.

"Pull over, pull over!" she kept saying to me.

"I can't," I said. "I've got to get home to my kids."

"We'll follow you."

For some reason they followed me home and helped me into my single-family house near CA 22, or locally known as the Garden Grove freeway. I walked in and my daughters started screaming. They helped me to the bathroom. When I looked in the mirror I knew why they were screaming: my face was covered in blood.

There was blood running out of cuts above my eyes. My upper lip had a hole in it and was nearly split. My eyes were puffing up and starting to close. My girls helped me wash up and put ice on my face.

My neighbor Jack came over and he called the cops to report what Glenn had done. I put a restraining order out on Glenn just in case. I later learned that Glenn skipped town.

It was weeks before my face and black eyes were presentable enough to be out in public. As a checkout clerk at Lucky's grocery store I had to face the public. When I did go back to work, I wore sunglasses so I wouldn't scare the customers.

The past is past and tonight I'm just a thirty-two-year-old mother of four sitting in a bar waiting for her husband to show up.

CHAPTER 2

Feeling No Pain

I sipped my beer and looked around the busy pool hall waiting for Ron to arrive. He said he would meet me here. I needed to see Ron. I knew I still loved him; I've been in love with him ever since that first kiss in my kitchen.

A guy walking by gave me a second look. People say I look like the movie star Ann-Margret with my green eyes and red hair, and I've never weighed more than one hundred and twenty-five pounds, which I thought was fat on my petite frame.

One day when I was at Lucky's doing my check-out clerk job, a dad and his young son came through my line. The kid was looking at the magazines and Ann-Margret happened to be on the cover of one of them. He said to his father, "Look, Daddy, this lady's picture is on the magazine!"

It sure made me feel good. I just wished I had felt that pretty inside.

As a kid I was always looking for my father's affection. I never got it despite trying real hard to be good in school and taking care of the house. I guess I just wasn't good enough to deserve his affection.

I worked at the cash register because it was one of the only jobs I could get. I had dropped out of high school at age fifteen when I discovered I was pregnant.

My boyfriend Wayne asked me to marry him. I was only sixteen and he was twenty. Four years later I was still a wife and mother and we had three kids. I thought life was great. But Wayne was addicted to alcohol and drugs and then he started to physically abuse me.

Wayne and I were driven apart by the drugs, alcohol, and abuse, and so I sought solace in another man: Ron. I had an affair with Ron and he fathered my fourth child, a beautiful baby boy, while I was still married to Wayne. I filed for divorced because I couldn't hide the bruises on my face anymore.

After the divorce, Ron moved into my house and four years later Ron and I went to Las Vegas and got married. We were married two years, but had separated recently. Ron hadn't moved out all of his belongings because he did a lot of traveling as a truck driver. The problem was I still loved him, and right now I needed to see him. So here I am drinking a beer waiting for Ron.

Ron walked into the bar.

"Ron, I've missed you," I said, giving him a big hug. He hugged me right back and gave me a big old kiss.

We grabbed some fresh beers and took a pool table and started playing. We were having a grand old time trying to best each other at pool. We were laughing, playing pool, and drinking just like the old days.

After playing pool we went to the bar and sat. We were drinking and talking with this guy next to Ron. His name was Jim. We talked about every subject, including guns.

"I've got a collection of guns," said Jim. He said one of his guns was a .22 caliber nickel-plated, long-nosed revolver.

Ron and I exchanged looks. We used to have a gun collection, including a revolver that matched this description, but it had been stolen from our house just a couple of years ago. Naturally, we wondered if Jim's long-nosed revolver was one of ours. We didn't have any way of knowing until we actually examined it. We didn't mention our suspicions to Jim. At closing time, Jim invited us back to his house to look at his collection. Well, of course we agreed.

Ron went ahead with Jim. I made the short drive home to Lariat Street to check on the kids and tell them where I was going.

Kim, my fifteen-year-old daughter, knew I had been drinking; she didn't want me behind the wheel of a car because she knew my wild, drunken past.

"Mom," she said. "You should really stay home."

"I'll be okay. I'll be safe with Ron," I said and left the house.

CHAPTER 3

Is That Ours?

Jim's house was only fifteen minutes away. By the time I arrived, Jim had already placed a number of handguns on the coffee table. Ron was sitting in an easy chair. I took a seat on the couch facing Ron and the coffee table was between us. Jim excused himself and left he room.

I leaned over and picked up the .22 caliber, long–nosed revolver with the hair trigger; it looked just like the one we once had in our collection. We had it until my ex-brother in-law Raymond had stolen our collection from us, or at least I suspected he was the one who stole it. The police never caught him on that charge.

I looked at the plating, the barrel length, and the barrel, and cocked the hammer back. After looking the gun over and feeling its weight, I put the gun back on the coffee table. I settled on the couch and got a cigarette out. I put the cigarette in my mouth and was searching for a match when I heard a sharp cracking sound.

My right arm suddenly felt like it was on fire. I felt a burning in my chest. A tingle was boiling in both of my feet. I looked at Ron.

Ron was holding the long-nose revolver that I had just put down. He was sitting in the deep chair on the other side of the coffee table. He looked startled. He quickly put the gun down.

Horror engulfed me; I couldn't move my legs! I had a fleeting thought about what someone had once said about being paralyzed. I knew I had been shot.

"I think you hit me," I cried out.

"I didn't shoot you," said Ron. "There's no blood."

I looked down at the flowered blouse I was wearing over a brown turtleneck. There was a small, dark red, wet spot on my left chest near a tear in my blouse. No blood was gushing.

Jim ran into the room. "What happened?"

"Jesus, Jim," said Ron jumping up and pointing to the gun. "This thing is loaded!"

"Of course it's loaded," Jim assured him. "It's the one my wife keeps in the bedroom dresser for protection."

I was still looking down at the blood spot, thinking it was weird there wasn't a lot more blood.

Then I felt a thousand needle pricks rising up my legs and arms. My breathing became short and shallow. I was scared. The tingling reached my shoulders. I could feel the panic rising within me as well. The tingling reached my throat.

"Ron, I can't feel my legs," I cried before everything went black.

CHAPTER 4

What Happened?

I blinked my eyes hard a couple of times, trying to focus. I could hear muffled activity of some sort, and a murmur of voices. When my eyes focused I saw the ceiling. It wasn't my bedroom ceiling but it was a familiar ceiling. It was a hospital ceiling.

What was I doing in a hospital?

I heard crying. I tried to speak but my voice didn't come out right. Ron came into my line of sight.

"Why am I here?" I asked, my voice just a whisper.

"I'm so sorry, I'm so sorry," he said wiping tears from his eyes.

I wanted to hold him but I was so tired I couldn't move a muscle.

"After you collapsed Jim and I rushed you to the hospital and we called for a gurney and they didn't think you were going to make it and I couldn't live without you and doctors said they would try but they didn't know."

"Slow down. Start again," I croaked.

Ron took a big breath.

"After you collapsed, Jim suggested calling an ambulance. I said there was no time for an ambulance, so the two of us carried you to the car and drove as quickly as possible across the street to the hospital.

"Once we got to the ER someone brought a wheelchair but I said you'd been shot and couldn't sit up. They wheeled you in on a gurney to a cubicle where a doctor cut off your blouse and turtleneck." He stopped to wipe his eyes and nose.

"Then the doctor turned to me and asked me, 'You don't expect me to save this woman, do you? The bullet has gone through her lungs!'"

Ron started crying. "I'm so sorry. The doctor told you to keep breathing and you kept breathing. Then when they put a tube in the side of your chest a rush of blood shot across the room," Ron took a couple of breath. "I guess I passed out at that point."

"I was shot?"

"Remember we were looking at guns with Jim?"

I concentrated. I remembered the pool hall, playing pool and drinking, but vaguely remembered looking at or handling some guns.

Ron continued, "You put a gun down and I picked up the gun and when I sat down it went off."

"And then?" I asked.

"Well, here you are."

"You shot me?"

"I'm so sorry; I didn't mean to do it. The gun just went off."

"It's okay," I said looking into his red eyes.

"When did you shoot me?"

"Saturday night."

"What day is it?"

"It's Monday," Ron said.

"I've been out of it for two days?"

"No," Ron said shifting his gaze away from me.

"Today is Monday, June 19th."

"June 19th?" June?

The last thing I remembered was drinking in the bar, but that was way back in April.

I've been in a hospital bed for two months?

What the hell happened?

I could feel the tears forming in my eyes. Ron moved out of my line of sight. I turned my head but I couldn't see him.

"Ron? Ron?" I wanted to get up and find him but I found it difficult to move. He wasn't there.

"I'm so glad you're awake," said a nurse, coming into view. "That's good. Don't struggle, dear."

"Where's Ron?"

"He stepped out. He's been here almost every day."

"What about my kids?"

"I don't know. You'll have to ask your husband or your parents. I'll let the doctor know you're awake."

I heard the door open and my parents walked in. We all started crying. They were glad to see me and I was glad to see them. Then the doctor came in.

He was looking at the chart.

"So what happened?" I asked.

"You're one lucky lady," he said. "Somebody upstairs must like you. Anyway, the bullet entered your left chest cavity below the heart and missed the heart. It traveled and hit your left shoulder blade, bounced into and through both lungs leaving two holes in each one, ricocheted off a rib and into your throat where it hit your spine. It still had enough power to shatter vertebrae and cut your spinal cord at cervical discs six and seven. They are right near the neck," he explained calmly. His hand went to my neck and I felt him feeling my neck.

"If it had been a larger caliber bullet, we wouldn't be having this conversation," he said.

"Why not?" I asked.

He looked away. "You and your family should prepare for major paralysis. It's been two months. It could be two more months, six months, or for life."

For life? I tried to move my toes but I couldn't feel them. I tried to move my fingers and some of them moved.

The doctor left.

CHAPTER 5

Wide Awake

My parents gave me a kiss and left.

I was awake now.

I contemplated what the doctor had said; paralysis might be for life. For life? I started to cry and then I cried some more.

"This just can't be happening to me, this can't be my life!"

I tried to distract myself by watching television, but all I could do was just lie there, asking myself over and over again, "How this could be happening to me?"

"What hospital am I in?" I asked the nurse when she came back.

"You're in Garden Grove hospital," she said.

I turned my head to watch her go and saw the nurses' station was near my room. The sign on the front of the desk said "ICU: Intensive Care Unit."

I was, and have been, in intensive care for two months. Now I was so tired I fell asleep thinking about looking at the guns on that night over two months ago.

When I woke up, I heard crying. I turned my head to the left and saw Ron sitting near me.

"Ron?" I said.

"Hi," he said, drying his eyes.

"I'm so sorry for putting you in here. It's entirely my fault."

"Don't be so hard on yourself," I said as I tried to recall some of the details of that night. "I must have flipped the safety off."

Truth be told I remember pulling the hammer back on the gun but I couldn't let my father know I did that! I was letting Ron take the fall.

"But it was in my hands," he sniffed. "I told the police what happened. I know they thought it was an accident too, but I shot you."

His conscience was bothering him bad. I knew it was an accident. I tried to reassure him that I was neither angry with him nor did I hold him responsible. In fact, I felt no anger toward him whatsoever.

I wiggled the fingers on my left hand to the edge of the bed to hold his hands. I still couldn't move my toes or my legs yet.

"How are the kids?"

"They're fine, they're with Linda," he said. That was my sister-in-law. "She volunteered to take them seeing she has kids of her own."

I looked at his eyes. They were red from crying, but the whites of his eyes were bloodshot. I bet he had been drinking. He was sober now, but he was drinking, I could tell.

"It must be hard for her," I said.

"With her kids it is," Ron said. "But she's glad to do it."
Ron stayed for a while.

When my parents showed up, Ron started to leave. As I watched him and my parents cross paths, I could see there wasn't any love lost between them.

"That man should be in jail for what he did to you," said my father.

"Dad, it was an accident," I said.

"He shot you. He admitted it."

"He didn't mean to shoot me. The gun had a hair trigger."

"He shot you, and that's all there is to it," my dad insisted.

My dad was a hard man. Getting married at sixteen got me out from under his domination. I could never do anything right: in school my grades weren't high enough, as a cheerleader I wasn't cheery enough, and my house cleaning skills weren't good enough. Wayne, my first husband, thought I was pretty and loved to touch me tenderly, and I fell for him. But, Ron loved me, and I loved him.

"How are you feeling today?" my mother asked.

I had started to move my arms and fingers but that was it. Thank God for my mother. She has been an inspiration and a friend to me. Seeing me like this must have been a disappointment for her. At least she didn't say anything bad about Ron.

"I'm praying for you dear," my mother said, giving me a kiss.

My mother and grandmother have always prayed. They helped instill in me my belief in God.

My parents were so nice to come and see me. But they and Ron never came at the same time and that hurt me.

CHAPTER 6

Ron Goes to Rehab

"I'm going away," Ron said one day, as he sat by my bed.

"Driving?" He drove long-haul trucks.

"No," he said. "Rehab."

"Oh," I said. He was going to get clean and sober? Thank God. Alcohol had been driving us apart. I went to AA last year to get sober, and I stayed with it because I loved that God was part of it. Ron only came one night. He had been sober for twenty-four hours and during the meeting he went into a convulsion. That was the last time he went. I hoped his rehab time would get him right because I needed him now more than ever.

"I got to go," he said. "I'll write you."

Two days later I received the first letter from him.

The nurses came in to care for my body every day. I had an in-dwelling urinary catheter and a bed pan because I couldn't tell if I had soiled myself or not. It was embarrassing having someone clean me, but what was worse is that I didn't feel it—none of it. I couldn't sit up or move my legs. I couldn't see if my toenails needed clipping or if my legs needed shaving.

Then they gave me medication for pain and depression.

"Why do I need antidepressants?" I asked the nurse.

"The doctor feels you'll adjust better if you stay upbeat."

I was crying, and I didn't see how that was upbeat. I didn't want to be paralyzed. I wanted my old life back.

I found out that it's common practice for almost all newly paralyzed patients to receive antidepressants. The new reality that paralysis brings makes many patients suicidal unless they have some way to dull the horror.

My depression was deepened by the behavior of my well meaning parents who treated me like a child again. They no longer believed I was a capable adult, presuming that since I had lost the ability to take care of myself—much less my children—I was just like a child. My body may have been lifeless like a little baby, but my mind was still functioning like an adult. I was determined to prove them wrong.

My good friend Marilyn came to visit.

"Have you seen my kids?" I asked her.

"Yes, they are doing well but it's tough on Linda and Dave. The kids are out of their element there too."

"What can I do? I can't come home yet. Ron went off to rehab. I don't want to burden my parents with them, or should I say, burden my kids with my father."

"I could take care of the kids at your house until you get home," she said.

"That's a good idea," I said. "The kids can be home. Are you sure you want to take this on?"

"Sure."

With Ron in rehab, I gave Marilyn power of attorney so she could pay bills and take care of the household. I had been in the hospital's ICU for three months and now California Social Services wanted to take my kids away and send them to different homes. They felt that we couldn't be good parents to our kids because I was paralyzed and Ron was in rehab. That was something I couldn't allow them to do.

I refused to give my kids up. My father went to court for me and pleaded my case, and he won. I won the right to have my kids stay together. If it hadn't been for my dad, and for Marilyn's kindness and compassion and taking my kids from Linda's care, the kids would have been separated.

Marilyn worked at her job during the day. My oldest daughter, Kim, watched her younger siblings after they all got out of school. When Marilyn finished work, she returned to the house to take over from Kim and spend the night making sure the kids were safe.

I missed Ron terribly but I was glad he was getting help for his drinking problem. I wrote back to Ron every time he wrote to me. It was so good hearing from him and to read in his letters of how much he loved me, how much he had enjoyed making love to me, and how he was looking forward to that again. Our lovemaking had been great, and I was looking forward to his caresses again.

Our letters were filled with the longings we had for each other. Our relationship had always been very physical. I loved it when Ron wrapped his strong body builder arms around me at night, even if we were just watching television.

"You sure do mail a lot of letters to Ron," Marilyn said one day after I handed her another envelope.

"We're still married, even though I'm here and he's in rehab." I said. "I still love him."

"It's lucky that he's in rehab," she said, getting up. "He could have been thrown in jail."

"What do you mean?" I asked.

"After the shooting, the cops found out he had an existing warrant," she said pausing, then looked at me. "The judge gave him a choice of jail or rehab. I'm sorry."

I thought Ron had gone into rehab to help himself and to save our marriage? I truly thought he would quit drinking, help with the children, and help me adjust to a completely different existence. I guess I was wrong.

CHAPTER 7

God's Will

During one of my parents' visits, I talked to my father about God.

I knew he had been praying for me to walk again, despite his being an atheist. It broke my heart that his disbelief became stronger and more solidified after his prayers appeared to go unanswered.

"Your prayers have been heard," I said. "I've been taken care of." I knew God was taking care of me the whole time. "Neither you nor I can truly know what God's plan is or the purpose of my paralysis in the big picture."

Dad would hear none of that kind of talk. It was cut and dried as far as my dad was concerned: God didn't do what he asked Him to do, so he gave up on God.

"Don't you know, Dad, that God is the reason I'm alive today? Remember when the doctors told Ron in the emergency room that there was no way I was going to make it?" I reminded him. "Instead of dying, I'm here today. All these months I've been fighting. Now something helped me along and I know it was God!"

"What god would let you lie there like that?" he angrily countered. "I prayed my heart out the night you were shot and asked the Lord to let you walk."

"Sometimes we don't get what we pray for, Dad," I softly responded. "I know there is a reason I'm this way. I don't know what it is or how well I'm going to accept this throughout my life, but I'm going to do my best. Maybe I'm supposed to show somebody else something or help someone else. I don't know. I just know there's a bigger picture."

Despite my impassioned words, he didn't buy any of it. I knew he was not the kind of person who could be pushed into things. I tried hard, without pushing, to bring God into the conversation in whatever situation we found ourselves in. I couldn't give up on my dad.

CHAPTER 8

Visitors Aren't Always Welcome

While I was in the ICU, many people came to visit me, but since the hospital didn't welcome a lot of visitors in my room, my isolation magnified my depression. I profoundly missed my children. I wondered how I was going to take care of them as a parent should, and yet I wondered how I could even begin to face them in my condition. My parents thought I was a child again so what would my children think?

I had been listless until the doctor gave my parents' permission to bring my four children to the hospital's ICU. Their visit brought me out of my fog and back into consciousness. Kim was fifteen, Kevin, fourteen, Kari, twelve, and Paul was seven. All I wanted to do was go home to the kids, but I couldn't even sit up yet. How was I going to take care of them? It was so good to see them. They were my life. They gave me strength when I felt weak.

Kim told me that back in April, it had seemed strange that when she woke up, I hadn't returned home and I didn't leave a note or anything, and then Linda came to the door and told them what had happened.

The folks at Lucky's, the grocery store where I used to work, raised money for me and in the process, made many aware of my accident. As a result, the walls of my hospital room were covered with cards from people, some of whom I had never met.

One day when I opened my eyes, Glenn was there holding two dozen red roses.

"I'm sorry about the shooting," he said.

"Thank you."

"If I hadn't hit you, you would have still been with me and not Ron. You wouldn't have been shot."

I just stared at him. How could he even say that?

"You aren't responsible for anything that's happened to me," I said. "You don't have anything to do with my life.

Now leave before I call the cops again." I had called the cops when he beat me bloody for breaking up with him. He turned like a wounded beast and slunk out of the room.

He came back another time with two dozen roses. I didn't give him a chance to say anything; I just yelled at him to get out.

Ron's parents came to see me in the hospital. They looked sad when they saw me.

Ron's dad looked me right in the eye and asked "How are you able to go to the bathroom?"

I couldn't believe he would ask such a personal question. It was bad enough that I couldn't tell when I went and needed someone to clean me, but to have him ask me that as an opening line just irked me to no end.

One person who didn't come see me at Garden Grove Hospital was my ex-husband Wayne. I thought he would stop by, seeing as I was the mother of his three children. I thought he would be concerned, but then again, he was more concerned with getting drunk or getting his next fix and running with the boys than caring about me. The last time I was in the hospital and he came to see me, it wasn't very pleasant.

It was seven years ago, just four months after Paul was born. My marriage to Wayne had deteriorated and Ron and I were having an affair. I was helping Ron with his truck's paperwork and occasionally riding with him. One night Ron was driving his truck while I followed in my mom's car. We hit a newly oiled patch of road and I lost control of the car and rolled the car off the road. I was brought to the hospital and the hospital staff called my husband, Wayne.

Wayne came to the hospital and found out that I had been with Ron.

Wayne proceeded to wrap his hands around my throat right there while I lay in my hospital bed. The nurses called security. They were able to get him off me and kept him from killing me.

CHAPTER 9

I'm Stable Enough

I told every nurse, visitor, and especially my parents, that Ron was guilty of nothing. I explained that I had probably, unknowingly, set the hair-trigger on the gun, making it ready to discharge.

Despite my continued love for Ron and my fervent defense of him, my parents grew to hate him, blaming the shooting on him. My parents weren't the only ones who believed Ron shot me on purpose. After all, everyone knew we were separated and how jealous Ron was. The fact that he was innocent didn't change many people's minds. It was a tough situation for Ron to live with, which only exacerbated his self-hatred.

One day while my folks were with me in the hospital, my father put his hand on my foot and it moved. All three of us rejoiced, thinking it was a sign the paralysis was reversing. My father excitedly called the doctor to witness the miracle.

The doctor made the sorry announcement that spasms occur regularly in newly paralyzed people; it was not necessarily a sign of good news. As far as he was concerned, it was still a waiting game.

My mother and I prayed for my recovery.

I was now able to use my arms and prop myself up when needed. I was even able to use a wheelchair, but I needed help getting into the chair. But I was still basically unable to care for myself.

In July, three months after the shooting, I was stable enough to be transferred from Garden Grove Hospital to the spinal cord rehabilitation center at Rancho Los Amigos in Downey, California. The good news was that at Rancho I could have as many visitors as I wanted.

CHAPTER 10

Grueling Rehabilitation

At Rancho I was put in a co-ed room with six beds. All the rooms in this section were co-ed. I didn't mind the company, but I didn't think about the consequences.

After settling in, the Rancho doctors took me off all the drugs I had been receiving while at Garden Grove Hospital. I had been on antidepressants and other drugs for nearly three months. Now suddenly, I was without them. I endured two weeks of pain and suffering as I went cold turkey, but at the time I was unaware that this was a result of drug withdrawal.

I, and everyone in my room, was relatively helpless. While we were there to learn how to function again, we were dependent upon the staff for critical help in moving and personal care.

I discovered the staff were frequently insensitive and turned a deaf ear to our requests. Staff members yelled at me and other patients. They told us dismissively that they'd take care of us "when they had time," only to turn on their heels and disappear. For me it was a nightmare existence where no staff person had compassion for my plight. I thought they would have more pity on me than I had on myself because they worked at a rehabilitation center, but I was wrong.

I was furious about the treatment meted out to me and the other paralyzed patients. I felt staff members were flat out mean as they pushed us patients around. I felt debased knowing I was helpless to do anything about it. Doctors, who came in only once a week, were pretty much unaware of the frightening so-called care doled out by the rank and file staff at Rancho.

Like I said, I was in a co-ed room, and I didn't mind being in the company of other patients. But I did mind being denied privacy and consideration when I was undressed. Can you imagine having your clothes changed or being washed without having privacy curtains? I was humiliated by the insensitive treatment. I felt like an object being worked on. I felt utterly dehumanized.

Nevertheless, I drew on my inner reserve, vowing to be my own advocate and to do as much for myself as I possibly could, as soon as I could. I knew that if I were to keep my children, I would need to learn how to do my laundry and other ordinary household duties.

When I was able to, I took my own laundry down to the laundry room to do it myself. For this achievement I was praised, and because of my strong determination I was in good stead.

I, of course, was not the only one at the Center challenged by paralysis. One of my roommates at Rancho was a fifteen-year-old girl from Missouri who had jumped off a rock at a swimming hole, hit her head and broke her neck. She was now paralyzed from the neck down.

Another fifteen-year-old girl in my room suffered the same level of paralysis as me. I thought this girl was a tough kid, but had been spoiled prior to her accident. Nonetheless, this young girl showed her mettle daily as she worked diligently to rehabilitate herself. Of course, she had her down times like anyone else, but I was inspired by her ability to deal with her situation.

The reason we were all at Rancho was to learn how to use our bodies again.

The staff inflicted an inflexible schedule on us. Everyone was forced to get up at seven, wash themselves, and go workout all day.

One of our goals was to regain our balance. I learned that people who lose their spinal cord fluid, lose their sense of balance too. We were like babies all over again and we had to be taught how to sit up. When we learned to sit up we then had to learn balance. I and the others would sit on a great big rubber mat while the therapists threw big beach balls at us trying to knock us over. Because everyone was in the same boat, we'd fall over erupting with laughter about our shared plight.

Little by little, as my balance improved, I was getting better at catching the ball rather than being bowled over by it. After practicing hard every day, I could eventually sit up and catch the ball without a problem. The feeling of triumph was incredible.

One August morning, I heard one of the teenage girls crying because a therapist wanted to get her up, but she didn't want to as long as there were boys in the room. I thought the head of physical therapy was nothing but a little twit who would lord over his patients with his tidbit of power. Scant though it was, he used his power like a bludgeon. He started yelling and cursing the girl.

"You god damn spoiled brat!" he hurled at her. By this point, both fifteen-year-old girls were hysterical. Even their mothers, who were there at the time, were crying.

I was furious. After all, I was the mother of a fifteen-year-old. I had seen these two mothers put on brave smiles, showing upbeat attitudes every moment they were with their daughters. But I had often found them both in the hallway drowning in tears. I had a great deal of empathy for these mothers and what they were going through.

"Thank you, God," I said. "That this has happened to me and not my daughters." I couldn't imagine how I could handle it if it were Kim or Kari here instead of me.

This gratitude for my daughters being okay was pivotal for me. It helped me accept my condition. Just watching these poor mothers keep a smile on their faces and then go out in the hall to break down in private put it all in perspective for me.

After the arrogant, offensive head therapist had screamed at the two girls, he left the room. I got into my wheelchair, and just happened to roll my wheelchair up beside him. He was in the snack area to have a cup of coffee. He was bitching and cursing loudly to an assemblage of nurses about his run in with the girls.

"Do you know what?" I queried. "I've been here for months, and I've watched you train people in physical therapy. You are grand at what you do. You know exactly what to do when it comes to physical therapy. But you don't know what you're doing when it comes to relating to human beings. Those girls in there are children who have just found out that they'll probably never be mommies, never be married, and never fulfill their dreams. Yet you go in there and attack those children. I think it's a disgrace. Do you do such things because it makes you feel like a big man?" I demanded.

Once I let the first words out I began to cry. The man was totally silent as I got a cup of coffee and rolled myself back to my room. Speaking up on behalf of those girls—

and all the patients that would follow—was a red-letter day for me. I felt good about speaking up.

I was especially heartened to note a pronounced change in the demeanor and attitude of the head physical therapist after I let him have it. The taste of self-empowerment and the knowledge that I had the ability to make a positive difference were heady.

Our daily routine included weight lifting. All of the paraplegic patients worked out with weight machines in the gym. We had to strengthen whatever muscles we still had control over. Each day I lifted weights to build my upper body strength. I had to learn a long list of physical actions before I could go home, such as rolling over, scooting around by using my arms, and transferring into a car, a bed, or a chair—actions that I had taken for granted when I could use my legs.

They pushed us, and it was hard work. In the beginning I couldn't stop crying. I cried because the work was so hard. I cried because I wanted to be with my children. I cried because sometimes I lost the will and desire to live.

Not only did the bullet paralyze me below the waist, but it also destroyed a nerve that ran down my right arm into my right thumb, index and middle fingers. Because

I couldn't bend those fingers, I couldn't grip anything. So part of my rehabilitation involved hooking a little mini rug of sorts. I had to poke a needle through holes and then use the fingers on my right hand to pull the shag rug material through the holes. I was left-handed, but they still wanted me to regain dexterity in those fingers on my right hand.

Learning how to get dressed was one critically important part of rehabilitation. The staff wanted to watch me get dressed but, I was greatly insulted if a staff member stood by watching me as I attempted to dress. I didn't want an audience.

"Give me my clothes, close the curtain and I'll let you know when I have them on," I insisted. My dignity was on the line.

Despite protestations by the staff that I was supposed to be observed during the process, they finally relented after I threw a fit.

"I can do it!" I emphasized.

From that landmark day on, I was able to dress myself successfully.

I also resisted what they called "toilet training." When I went into the bathroom the first time, I reeled from the smell and the filth.

"If you think I'm sitting on one of these toilets, I've got news for you. I'm NOT! Somebody is going to have to come in here and clean one of them with bleach before I'm ever going to use the toilet."

A little bleach along with some moping and scrubbing could have converted the filthy bathroom to a clean one. I couldn't believe a state-sanctioned hospital had such unsanitary conditions.

"You're just stubborn," said the aide.

"I never let my bathrooms at home get this filthy, and I have four kids!" I said. I just wanted the bare necessities of decent care, and my protests were rewarded with improved conditions.

Rancho also offered instruction on how to drive a car using hand controls to those who were interested and wanted more independence. I jumped at the chance.

I've always loved cars and really got into them when I was a teen. I owned a sports car that was designed by Ford to be a race car: my 1970 Mustang Mach One. Just thinking of that blue car decked out with a black racing stripe and an all-white leather interior still thrills me.

I remember the thrill I got from the four-speed shift and the powerful 351 engine equipped with a hood scoop over the carburetor.

I have fond memories of my cars.

I've got pictures of almost every car I ever owned and pictures of the kids and me going through the giant redwood tree that you can drive through. The kids always wanted to go there, drive through the tree and have their pictures taken with me, the car, and the tree. Those are great memories.

So I took the driving course and learned how to drive with hand gears.

CHAPTER 11

Sexual Frustration

My daily physical therapy routine went on for two and a half months.

I was still dismayed, however, by my parents' inability to treat me as an adult. I closely identified with the movie, "Born on the Fourth of July," that starred Tom Cruise. He played Ron Kovac, a Marine who became a paraplegic fighting in the Vietnam War. According to the movie, Kovac had a very difficult time once he came home because his family treated him like a child. I was told this was par for the course, but I railed at their attitude.

Here I was, thirty-two years old, yet my parents simply could not accept that I was still an adult in a paralyzed body. Understandably, they cried all the time, which made it even more difficult for me to accept my condition.

My mom visited me quite often, and while she struggled to accept what had happened, she was able to. My dad visited only on the weekends, and he had a hard time adjusting. I guess he figured that because my body was as immobile as a child, my brain must be too. His attitude drove me crazy.

Books, therapists, and conversations with other paraplegics confirmed to me that the panic about losing the ability to have and enjoy sex was almost universal. I was no exception. This situation was illustrated in the movie "Born on the Fourth of July" when friends take Kovac to a house of ill repute to jump-start his sexual engine.

After I had been at Rancho for a while, I was able to leave on a pass because I could manage my body. By this time Ron was out of rehab, so he took me home for the evening so I could see the kids. Of course, since we were still married, it never crossed my mind that I would have to tell my parents where I was going or with whom. I was just living like a married adult woman. Sexuality had always been important to me, so it was only natural that I'd want to give my new body a go with my husband.

Once home, I hugged and talked to my children. It was glorious to be with them. After the kids went to bed, Ron took me to the bedroom, placed me on the bed, and took the phone off the hook.

I was deathly afraid I'd be unable to participate in sex, but I had to know if I could. While Ron had been in rehab, his daily letters to me often talked about his desire to have sex with me again as he reminisced about our mutually delightful sexual relations.

But the past was, well, past, and now I was concerned that sex might feel different to Ron. What if sexual intimacy with me didn't please him anymore? If it didn't feel good to him, would he still accept me as a woman?

If Ron failed to accept me, then who would ever accept me sexually since I was now living life in a wheelchair?

But the two of us were like kids, playfully re-exploring our sexuality. Much to my great relief, everything went well and Ron expressed his genuine pleasure about making love with me. The assurance that he still desired me thrilled me to no end. We ended up happily falling asleep in each other's arms.

In the morning, it didn't take long until our smiles turned to frowns because it wasn't like before; I didn't live at home. I was a patient at Rancho, and I was supposed to have returned to Rancho by 7 p.m. We had planned to get back in time; instead, we fell sound asleep and didn't wake up until morning.

By now, I'm sure the staff members at Rancho had tried calling, tried to get through, and couldn't because Ron hadn't put the phone back in the cradle. I knew I had to get back. Ron and I readied ourselves. I said goodbye to the kids, and we rushed out of the house.

As we were getting into Ron's car, my father's car came to a stop in front of my house.

My father? He lived forty miles away and he was here?

Did Rancho call him? He didn't look happy.

"You are trash," he began yelling at Ron. "An animal that you would have sex with my daughter in her condition is unthinkable." Then he turned to me.

"If you accept that man in your bed now that you're paralyzed, that means you don't appreciate a single thing your mother and I have done for you."

At this point, I truly hated my father for the terrible things he was saying and thinking. I had hated him off and on for years, mostly because I could never gain his approval. Now his words haunted me, and I started to question myself. Was it wrong for me to have sex now that I was paralyzed? I couldn't imagine why that would be true, but I had to find out from an expert.

Once back at Rancho, I requested a session with the resident psychiatrist. I was so confused between my feelings for Ron and my father's furious words that I didn't know what was right and what was wrong. I also wanted my parents included in the session so this issue could be worked out. And I hoped the psychiatrist could help my parents understand that I was still an adult and that the wheelchair didn't have anything to do with that fact.

The conference with the psychiatrist was set for a Saturday. I asked the psychiatrist to help my dad understand that I needed to know if I was still a woman. I wanted help getting my parents to understand that I could still have some degree of independence and could still get around on my own without having to report to them. After all, I was a married woman with four children, not my parents' little girl any more. It was all so frustrating and aggravating.

When the time came for the meeting my father refused to attend or even enter the room.

"I don't need any god damn psychiatrist at my age and nobody's going to tell me how to think," he bellowed.

I was struck by the irony since all my life he had told my sister and me exactly how to think. Anger and resentment welled up within me.

I was angry and my mother was weeping when we met in the psychiatrist's office to explain what had happened. I told him that my father refused to join us, and I shared the horrible things he had shouted to Ron and me after he found out that Ron and I had sex. I cried out the story.

Suddenly, there was a sharp knock and the door flew open. My dad rushed into the room, his face red with fury. The psychiatrist, seeing how irate he was, tried to calm him down.

"Mr. Thomas, please take a seat," the psychiatrist said, as he started to explain that there were some things that needed to be discussed in order to help my dad understand his daughter's needs.

"I understand one thing: my daughter is married to an animal," he roared at the psychiatrist. "I just went into her room and read some letters I found in her drawers that are full of sexual innuendo! This is an outrage!"

He was outraged? I just glared at him.

"Mr. Thomas, you're the one who needs help, not Janice," the psychiatrist said.

This statement startled my father so much that he muttered, "What do you mean by that?"

"First of all," the psychiatrist affirmed, "a grown man does not go into his thirty-two-year-old daughter's room, go through her dresser, and read her mail. That's the sickest thing I've heard in my entire time here at Rancho. You are obviously the one with sexuality problems. You and your ignorant attitude are killing your daughter."

I was stunned that someone would talk to my father that way, even though my father needed to be talked to in that manner. Unfortunately, the words fell on deaf ears; they didn't seem to faze my father. But this was nothing new. In my experience, nothing ever changed him. He said and did what he thought was right and that was that.

CHAPTER 12

Finally Going Home

In October, six months from the day of the shooting, I was released from Rancho Los Amigos and free to go home.

Home!

I had dreamt of arriving home for good and now my dream was finally coming true.

Before leaving Rancho, the head physical therapist thanked me for "waking him up." He promised not to yell at anyone else ever again. I felt great satisfaction in having made a positive difference.

Ron came to Rancho to help me pack up my belongings and drive me home. Only once in six months had I been outside and that was for just a night. Now I was heading home and did not have to return to a facility. This new perspective made the highways and traffic during the thirty-five mile drive seem new to me too. It was new to me because physically I was now a new person.

My four children, along with my parents, were at the house when I arrived. I cried and kissed everyone right there on the sidewalk. My kids seemed older and taller than when I had last seen them. Then I was struck by how much my parents had aged.

The wear and tear on my mother was gradual and really didn't register with me until now. My dad had only come to visit on the weekends, but now I noticed how much his body had shrunk and how much gray hair he had acquired since the accident. It was obvious to me that my parents had suffered mightily during this ordeal. Still they were happy to see me finally come home.

After taking note of my parents' physical deterioration, I next noticed my house.

The outside of the house, including the eaves and the trim, was painted and there was a new roof. The garden had been redone and the lawn manicured. The old cement patio now had a cabana-type structure on it and there was even a ramp out the back door so I could get in and out in my wheelchair. Inside there were new bathroom floors. I was totally surprised by the transformation.

Dad had completely refurbished it. I was overwhelmed by this dramatic demonstration of his love for me. Of course, he never uttered the words, but his dedicated work spoke volumes. This was the closest I had ever come to feeling loved and cared for by him and that meant the world to me.

Now that I was home, I could be a mother again and I tackled the daily chores and duties eagerly. I was determined to live as normal and independent a life as possible. I took on as many chores as I could handle such as the family laundry, scrubbing the kitchen floor from my wheelchair, and more.

The only thing Ron seemed able to handle was a bottle of whiskey.

I had hoped his stint in rehab had put his drinking days behind him, but his self-loathing and self-hatred had the better of him and his drinking stressed me to the breaking point.

"I have to get through life this way now," I implored him. "I just cannot tolerate your drinking. You are going to have to stop because I need you in so many ways. I need your love, your support, and your help. I need you to be sober because even though I learned a lot in rehab, I still need emotional support since life is much harder now."

He didn't respond.

A week later Ron told me he was going to help some guy with a car.

When Ron didn't return home that night I became hysterical. I calmed down long enough to think and I decided Ron had probably gone to Jim's house—the guy with the guns. I asked Marilyn to drive me to Jim's.

Sure enough, Ron was there. When he came out to the car he knelt down by the opened front passenger door. I twisted around in the seat so I could face him.

"What are you doing to me?" I cried. "Isn't my paralysis enough for me to deal with?" I was hysterical with anger, rage, and humiliation.

"I can't stay," Ron whispered. "I can't watch you like this. I can't bear to look at you and know that I put you in that wheelchair. I have to get away. All I do is cry and if I weren't such a coward, I'd kill myself."

In a wild fury I began hitting Ron in the face with my fists. How dare he ignore me! Marilyn pulled me away from

Ron, shut my door, and drove off as I screamed and cried. How dare he get up and walk away! I was in tears for days. I was bedeviled by unanswered questions: How could he leave me if he loves me? How can I function alone without his help? Was there no end to this nightmare that had become my life?

I turned to booze for comfort. Night after night I would listen to Barbra Streisand records and I'd drink. I'd cry and drink, drink and cry. Eventually Kim or Kari would take the drink out of my hand and put me to bed for the night.

My depression was epic. Here I was, bound to a wheelchair for the rest of my life. My husband had abandoned me. I was now the sole caretaker of four children aged fifteen and under.

I couldn't work.

I had no money.

I wasn't driving.

I was in the darkest place I had ever been. I could see no hope.

I questioned myself. I cried. I was tormented. All thoughts led to the same place.

I made a plan for the day I would take my own life.

CHAPTER 13

Who's There?

"Can you take the kids for a few days?" I asked Marilyn. "I need some alone time."

"Sure," Marilyn said. We arranged for the kids to go with her.

Once the kids were safely at Marilyn's, I went to my room. I scooted myself to the edge of the bed. I had bottles of sleeping pills and pain pills. I was sure they would give me the peace I was looking for.

I downed a handful of each of the pills. I poured out more. Grabbing my glass I looked at the pills in my hands.

"Janice."

I stopped.

I looked around. The tone of the voice was loving, tender, and reassuring. I felt peaceful. I was also a little scared since absolutely no one was in the house with me.

Because I was feeling scared, I turned on the television.

I wanted some noise in the room. I needed to calm down. I didn't want to hear voices out of nowhere!

The second the television came on the screen was filled with a man holding a microphone.

"If you think life isn't worth living, please call the number on your television screen now."

I blinked. Was he talking to me?

I put the pills down and picked up the pink princess phone next to my bed and dialed the number. I explained to the compassionate person on the other end of the line that I was in the midst of taking pills to end my life. The person told me not to take the rest of the pills, and instead to please put them down and pray. I put the pills down.

We prayed.

We talked.

I came to the firm conclusion that I needed to live after all.

I believe that my life was saved by divine intervention; I had no doubt the voice I heard was that of Christ or an angel. As with all the car crashes I had survived, I survived once again.

The prayer ministry sent me a prayer book and after that I called my AA sponsor to start going to meetings again.

From that point on, my independent nature took over. I was more determined than ever to learn how to be as self-sufficient as possible while in a wheelchair. Even though my return home had been difficult—leaving me wondering if I could handle everything—I vowed to keep the family together, which meant I simply had to prove my ability to function as a parent.

A continual stream of visitors came to the house, which was a good thing because I got lots of attention, but having visitors was also stressful for me. It was challenging enough to learn how to get around my own house, take care of my immobile body, and learn how to be a single, paralyzed parent without worrying about being a courteous hostess as well. Nevertheless, I persevered and made the best of it.

My mother had modeled independence for me. I had watched her become a golf widow when Dad repeatedly went off to play eighteen holes. It was a passion my mother did not share and so it made no sense for her to tag along.

But things changed when my father became interested in flying. Mom's fury at being left behind when he golfed fueled her resolve to avoid a similar scenario while he went flying. So when he decided to buy an airplane to learn how to fly, Mom announced she would get her pilot's license too. She was determined not to be left home alone any more.

They both passed all the required tests to become licensed private pilots. They flew for over ten years, enjoying the airways.

Their flying days literally came to a crashing halt in Mexico. The plane they were flying unexpectedly got caught in an updraft and Dad lost control, sending the plane nose first into the runway. Dad broke his ankle and Mom broke her arm. This experience proved to be sobering for both of them, so they mutually agreed to call it quits as pilots.

So, I vowed to do all I could around the house. What I didn't expect was for my parents to be over at my house too.

Dad's presence was upsetting to the children because he rode the kids relentlessly about doing this and that and not doing this and that. Just as I was never able to please him, my children found it equally impossible to live up to his standards.

I was much more understanding because I had grown up with his attitude. I realized the kids were adjusting to a new life as well. While they did need to take over some of the chores, the whole rhythm, flow, and designation of household responsibilities still needed to be worked out.

Instead of motivating the children to do more, Dad's constant criticism only served to halt their progress, often driving the children to tears.

Kim did the lion's share of the work: cooking, laundry and house cleaning duties. She took out the trash and did the dishes every night. I tried to assign jobs to each of the other kids, but they squirmed out of their duties and Kim would just take over and do them rather than argue about it. Kim began keeping the house immaculate just as I and her grandmother had done before her.

Kevin, my oldest son, wasn't even in the house to lend a hand. Shortly after I came home, he moved to Arkansas to be with his father, Wayne, to avoid having to go to a juvenile detention home.

Kevin had a long history of doing strange and sometimes illegal things. As early as age seven, he would wander into houses just to "look around."

The first time, he trespassed into a house across the street from his school. Not long after that first incident, he and a seven-year-old boy broke into another.

He often got caught, was reprimanded, and sent home. He seemed to want to get caught because frequently he'd leave his name on a pad of paper in the house. I was baffled, helpless to know what to do or how to help him.

As the years went on, his problems escalated and he began using drugs.

Finally, out of desperation, I decided to send Kevin to Wayne. When I had talked with Wayne on the phone, Wayne said he was going to church. I was impressed by how good Wayne sounded. I decided it would help Kevin if he joined the church with Wayne. I also thought Kevin would benefit from a man's influence. I was grasping at straws trying to figure out a way to help my son.

So for the first year while I was adjusting to life in a wheelchair, Kevin was adjusting to a new home in a new state. Kari, my third child, was twelve and at home. She was extremely difficult for me to deal with. She seemed to have no sympathy or empathy for me, acting cocky and cantankerous. Kari had been ornery from age two. She had no trouble speaking up when she either didn't like something or didn't want to do something. She was headstrong; she had her own clear picture of how reality was supposed to look.

Ask any middle school teacher: twelve is a daunting age with or without an innate headstrong nature thrown into the mix. I had my hands full, of that there was no doubt.

Despite my cornucopia of challenges, I was still determined to succeed. I was not going to lose my kids to the State. I tried to do the cooking, cleaning, and all manner of regular household chores from my wheelchair, but it took time to figure out new ways to make it all happen.

One day I was potting flowers when the pot slipped from my hand and dropped to the floor.

"Why, God?" I cried out. "I was just trying to plant a flower!"

Why was everything so difficult?

As I sat with the broken pot of flowers in my hands, I remembered the times as a child when I'd sit and watch my grandmother plant flowers in her garden. I especially loved snapdragons and, of course, pansies. My grandmother, like my mother, would respond to my questions with a heartfelt acknowledgment of God.

"God made everything," my grandmother would remind me. "If you take the time to look at things carefully, you'll see what an unbelievable miracle everything is. Only a power like that could possibly create such things."

Spirituality was a driving force for me from the beginning. When I was growing up, I shared my interest in spirituality with my girlfriends.

"Oh, you can come to church with me on Sunday," they'd say, one by one.

My best friend was Catholic, but in those days the entire service was conducted in Latin and I didn't understand a word and I quickly lost interest. Next I attended a Lutheran church with another girlfriend, then later a Church of God. The frenzied outbursts at the Church of God freaked me out. People would jump up from their seats, lie on the floor, and scream a lot. Next was a Baptist church.

That was pretty much the full extent of my formal religious experiences during my childhood. God was firmly in my heart, regardless of what church I found myself visiting or not visiting.

I cleaned up the broken pot of flowers and set it aside.

CHAPTER 14

Tackling Housework

Not surprisingly, being paralyzed and wheelchair-bound brought on severe bouts of depression that slowed my life down considerably.

I still had the use of my shoulders, arms, hands, neck, and head.

My arms, hands, and shoulders got a tremendous workout just getting myself out of bed in the morning. The ordeal of washing and dressing took a good hour, not counting the time I spent doing my hair and makeup. Everyday chores like cooking, doing the dishes, and cleaning out the refrigerator and oven turned into brutal workouts.

Nonetheless, I gritted my teeth to get through it.

I simply felt I had to do it all.

My parents would come over almost daily with their well-intentioned desire to do it all for me. I needed them to understand that it was very important to me to prove to myself that I was still useful. Yet I couldn't get it through their heads that although I was crippled, I wasn't useless. This battle continued for the first eight months after I came home from Rancho.

Uncle Bill, my mother's brother, came to town for a visit. His wife had just died. He was very depressed, as was I. He wanted to forget about his grief for a while so he asked his sister (my mother), me and my kids to accompany him to Scotts Mills, Oregon to visit his son Ron for two weeks. Everyone jumped at the chance, except Kim who had a job and didn't want to leave town.

In June, nine months after coming home, we went to Oregon for a vacation. The total population of the tiny cowboy town of Scotts Mills, Oregon was about two hundred people. To me, Scotts Mills looked like a fairyland: everything was green! After growing up in parched Southern California, I immediately felt like I belonged here.

The post office and firehouse were on the same street— the only main street in town. The next towns over were not larger than one or two hundred people. One tiny town followed another like pearls on a necklace. In their midst stood The Markum Inn, located in the town of Marquam. It was famous for its burgers and steaks. Every weekend, people lined up all the way around the outside of the building waiting to get in to eat.

We stayed with my cousin Ron in his house on Grandview Avenue. Farmland adjoined his property on the right with a forest on the left. A waterfall was visible across the yard.

The beauty and serenity of Scotts Mills simply thrilled me and it was love at first sight. I thought to myself how much I'd love to live here. It took me only three days to decide to sell my house in California and move to Scotts Mills. I had a powwow with the children who all agreed; Scotts Mills was where they wanted to live as well.

During our visit we met two local brothers: Bill and Wayne Johnson. The two boys were the same ages as Kim and Kari.

To my delight I discovered a small two-story white farmhouse that was for sale, just down the street and up the hill from my cousin's house. As far as I was concerned, the house was perfect. I loved the views from the windows. After all, I thought, if I were going to spend my life in a wheelchair, it would be so wonderful to look out the window to see such breathtaking scenery.

I made an offer, securing the house without having to make a down payment. As there were so few people in Scotts Mills and the surrounding areas, there was no competition from others wanting to buy the house. Buyers were rare, which gave me the advantage of being able to make the purchase contingent upon selling my Garden Grove home.

Two weeks later we returned to Southern California. I told Kim that we were moving and she wasn't very happy. Then I told my father that the kids and I were moving to Oregon. Dad thought that I had lost my mind.

Undaunted by my dad's incredulity I put my house on the market and sold it two months later. The proceeds from the sale were exactly what I needed to buy the house in Scotts Mills.

In the process of simplifying my life, I sold the Lincoln—the monthly payments on the Lincoln equaled my new house payment—and bought a 1972 Monte Carlo. Thanks to a donation by a handicapped person through my church, I was given hand gears for the new car which enabled me to drive again. Driving was not easy. I really had to concentrate on switching my reflexes from my feet to my hands.

Not only had I fallen in love with the beauty of Scotts Mills but there was another benefit to moving a thousand miles away: I would be out from under my parents' thumbs. I saw this move as a fresh start. I would be establishing my own independence too.

In November, four months after our vacation in Oregon and after Kevin had moved back home, the four children and I officially moved to Scotts Mills, Oregon. My dad relented enough to help the process along, even renting a U-Haul trailer that he pulled behind my new Monte Carlo.

I enrolled Kim at Silverton High. The younger children went to Scotts Mills Elementary, which ranged from kindergarten through eighth grade. After eighth grade, students went directly to high school.

The kids loved our adorable two-story white farmhouse, complete with a garden and fabulous views. I had always wanted a two-story home. The rooms were smallish, but there were four bedrooms on the second floor for the children, and on the first floor there was a bedroom off the dining room for me.

Kim, Kevin and I worked together to paint the house a cheerful yellow and white.

I still wasn't driving much and I needed to get around, so I figured Kim, now sixteen, was the likely driver. However, she was still under age, as the age to drive without parental consent was eighteen. I found out that there was a special chauffeur's license they could give to kids at age sixteen. I went down and argued with the authorities that Kim needed a license to drive me around. After a while they saw my point and Kim got her license at sixteen. When it came to my kids I fought hard.

Everywhere I looked in Scotts Mills, I was transfixed by beauty. The scenery during the drive from the house to the nearest grocery store took my breath away. The two-lane roads wound through farmland and forests populated with old, gigantic trees. Brooks and rivers added more enchantment.

The move proved ideal for family bonding. The kids and I would stay up late each weekend night eating popcorn, watching television, and playing cards and games.

It was the first week in December and we'd been living in Scotts Mills for about a month when I had a sleepless night. About two o'clock in the morning I finally got up, giving in to my body's refusal to sleep. Silence enveloped me as I wheeled myself over to the window and lifted the shade.

For the very first time in my life I witnessed falling snow. It was the most beautiful thing I'd ever seen. The ground was covered in a dusting of snow and the trees were blanketed white while snow kept falling. I was so excited I couldn't keep the spectacle to myself.

I yelled to the children on the second floor to get up because it was snowing. They all came charging down the stairway laughing and tumbling with glee, eager to be the very first one to go outside.

We all played in the snow in the middle of the night, marveling at the magical snowflakes that kept falling. From that night on, I christened wintertime in Oregon as "God's beautiful mystery."

I didn't have snow tires for my wheelchair, just the regular thin wheels that made it hard to get traction in the snow. I was determined; I would power my way through the snow. It was tough on my arms and shoulders but I succeeded in traversing the snow successfully.

Growing vegetables is a popular pastime in Scotts Mills and when springtime came we happily joined in. Many of the locals raised cows and pigs too, to butcher to keep meat on the table. But the children and I quickly decided we could not raise animals with the intent of eating them. I was adamant; there was no way I could bottle feed a calf, looking into its big, brown eyes only to shoot it or have it killed. No way. No how. So we focused our efforts on growing veggies instead.

Since childhood I've had a soft spot in my heart for animals. I'd bring home every stray animal I could find. As a kid I lived in Long Beach, California. When my sister Charlene was eleven and I was five, we had a horse. Charlene rode all the time. The horse regularly threw her off its back, but she was unfazed; she'd just climb right back on.

I would watch my big sister on horseback and yearn for a chance to ride. I was small as a five-year-old but I figured out a way to mount the horse by using the fence rather than vaulting up from the ground. I didn't mind because I wanted to ride in the worst possible way.

One day I accidentally left the gate open and I was afraid the horse would take off, so from the chicken gate I jumped onto his back before he got away. The horse was unimpressed by the orders of a five-year-old, and taking advantage of his new freedom, he refused to go back into the pen. Off we went, and we ended up down the street in a neighbor's front yard, where the horse was happy to munch and graze.

Spying the horse, the neighbor lady came outside and asked me if I knew my home phone number. I quickly responded with my phone number. The neighbor called my mother to calmly announce that her child was outside on top of a horse who was happily eating her grass. She issued an invitation for Mom to come get us.

CHAPTER 15

Starting a New Life

I was grateful to have my kids, Uncle Bill and his sister, as well as our cousins all living in Scotts Mills because I was fairly timid about going out in public in the wheelchair. Having family around gave us an enjoyable social group before we made other friends in the area. At first we felt people avoided us because we were outsiders from California.

I started bonding with the people who worked at the grocery store. I didn't mention where I was from but instead I shared the fact that I had been a grocery store cashier for fifteen years. This news cemented the relationship with the group, and suddenly I had buddies. I also met other families at my children's school events.

Bill and Wayne Johnson were the first kids to visit us in the new house once we were settled. Kim was immediately smitten with Wayne, the taller of the two. Wayne was sixteen years old.

Fourteen-year-old Bill acted like he was smitten with me. He waited on me hand and foot, helping me as much as possible. Bill was my great champion. Whenever the family was going anywhere, Bill was the first to volunteer to push me. Bill and Wayne became part of the family, going everywhere we went.

The two brothers would help with chores, go with me to my doctor appointments, and take me to after-school or weekend events.

I may have been timid about going out in the wheelchair, but Bill helped me by encouraging me to go. I suffered from the thoughtless behavior of people who had fully functioning legs. People would push ahead of me in line at the grocery store or bank, even though clearly I had been there first. I felt people expected me to be flexible enough to let them go first. It happened time after time.

One of my favorite outings was to take the children to the movies. One night after a movie, Bill was pushing me in my wheelchair when a man stepped right in front of me.

By this time, Bill had had it up to his eyeballs with other people's rude behavior so he rammed the wheelchair into the back of the guy's ankle, hoping to hit a tendon. I winced because I knew the metal footplate could be an effective battering ram. When the man turned around to glare, Bill asked him what he had expected. Did he think I would just fly up in the air and turn around to get out of his way? He added that the man deserved to get hit for being so rude and thoughtless.

I warned Bill that he was going to get me sued, but Bill merely responded that people who behaved that way deserved it. He reassured me, saying he sincerely doubted anyone could sue me over being hit by a wheelchair footplate in the ankle!

One day Bill and Wayne took us to Silver Falls State Park in Silverton, Oregon. It was a thirty minutes car ride to the park and another twenty minutes by car to make the seven-mile trip to the parking lot, which was up on top of a mountain. Bill and Wayne wanted the family to experience the park trail that winds in front of and behind ten waterfalls. I thought it was the most awesome place I had ever seen in my whole life—even prettier than Scotts Mills, which was really saying something.

Bill, full of big ideas, was sure he could successfully push me up and down the trail. The South Falls are one hundred and seventy-seven feet high and are accessed by a narrow, steep path on the side of a cliff. The trail goes behind the falls, bringing you out the other side. Bill couldn't wait to show me this incredible view.

I protested, pointing out to Bill that the trail was really steep, but Bill assured me we could do it. So I let this four-teen-year-old boy with admirable confidence give it a shot. I wasn't sure why I was letting him do it but I did. His older brother Wayne stayed right with Bill and me. A couple of times Wayne had to steady me because the path was barely wide enough for my wheelchair.

Finally we reached the bottom of the trail, which led to the other side of the water fall, but the trail narrowed significantly at this point so we were forced to turn around and backtrack. I got a firsthand experience of what it must feel like to be a salmon swimming upstream. Bill, Wayne, and I, complete with wheelchair, were now going against the crowd, and we had to circumvent a continuous stream of tourists who were going down the hill as we were going up.

Despite the tough going, Bill, Wayne, and I kept our sense of humor and we laughed our way back to the parking lot.

I was most comfortable sticking with the kids. Kids didn't care about my paralysis; they accepted me the way I was.

My home became the center of social activities since my children and their friends hung out there. I loved it that way. I happily wheeled around the house doing housework while chatting with the visitors. Usually there were at least four to six kids in the family room. The house layout required I go through the family room to get to the kitchen and bathroom. I often brought in a big basket of clean clothes to fold while the children were watching a ballgame. I would sit there, chatting and folding clothes. I enjoyed the time spent in their company.

Neighbors wondered why on earth I welcomed all those kids into my home, day in and day out. When questioned, I'd just reply that I couldn't find an adult who was as accepting of me in the wheelchair as the children were.

When the sun went down my house was still a beehive of activity. I established my authority quickly. I trained the children well and everyone knew that when they came over, they had to take their shoes off and line them up against the wall. Often there would be a continuous line of shoes from the back hallway down into the family room.

The lineup of shoes was crucial so I could get by them in my wheelchair. I only had to throw a couple of fits until all my rules were obeyed. The kids understood that if they wanted to hang out at my house, they had to abide by my simple rules.

The kid population of the house would double on the weekends, since each of my four children would have at least one friend over at the house from nine o'clock Saturday morning 'til Sunday night. They would have showed up earlier than nine, but that was one of the rules: "not before nine a.m." The truth was I loved it like this. I knew exactly where my children were and I could enjoy both their company and their friends' company. It worked out perfectly.

The children reported that I was a frequent topic of conversation among their neighbors. No one could figure out why the children enjoyed being at our house so much. They wondered if drugs were involved, but of course there were none.

I did allow my young visitors who were staying the night to drink beer at the house. I would call the parents too.

"If you don't want your child to be part of this, tell me now and then tell your child," I'd say to their parents. Invariably parents would say it was just fine. I got the feeling that the parents were grateful to have their children out of their hair. I loved having the kids around and didn't share the attitude of the other parents one little bit.

CHAPTER 16

My Teenagers

Back when I became pregnant by Ron, I was still married to Wayne. I was secretly thrilled to be carrying Ron's child. My intuition told me it would all work out in the end. I had some anxious moments during the pregnancy, no question about it, because Wayne thought it was his child and if I told him different I believed he would have killed me. He never guessed he wasn't the biological father.

Our son Paul was an easy child from the moment he was born in January 1968. He was a mild-mannered child and good looking to boot. Nothing about Paul was difficult. Paul was eight when we moved to Scotts Mills in 1976. It was the perfect environment for him to flourish. He loved the outdoors so much that I had difficulty convincing him to come inside for dinner.

Paul loved to spend time by the little pond behind our house, but when it froze over in the winter, he became concerned about the welfare of the carp that lived in the pond. One day in the dead of winter, I heard a knock at the back door. I opened the door to find Paul and a buddy standing there holding a huge, round piece of ice they had liberated from the pond. While I was looking at this unusual sight, I noticed all the dripping grass and fronds hanging from the bottom of it. As far as I was concerned, it was the ugliest thing I had ever seen, but I kept that opinion to myself.

Paul earnestly pleaded with me to put his treasure in the freezer. Of course, it was the last thing I wanted in the house, let alone the freezer.

"The grass that is hanging from the bottom of the ice is what the fish eat, so you'd better put it back," I said. That's what the little boy needed to hear. He wouldn't have done anything to deprive the fish of their next meal, so he and his friend marched it over to the pond and put it back.

As the kids grew older they presented more challenges for me. Their rooms were on the second floor and I couldn't climb stairs. Paul's room was located near the corner of the L-shaped house between the kitchen and the porch. A beautiful, big cherry tree grew near his window.

When Paul was in high school, his engaging personality, good looks, and long eyelashes made him the object of many girls' romantic fantasies. The girls' pursuit of Paul went on for quite some time before I became aware of their ardor and their ability to climb the cherry tree.

One morning I was stunned to see a girl come down the stairs with a head of hair the size of a basketball. It was the biggest hair I've seen in my entire life. She looked like a giant hairball going out the door!

Naturally I called Paul downstairs to find out who that was and what she was doing in the house. Paul informed me that she said she was in love with him and that he had a big challenge fending off her kisses and advances! That didn't explain why she was coming down the stairs.

Girls weren't the problem with Kevin, however. Drugs were. By age thirteen he started drinking and taking drugs. I noticed his behavior had changed and that he was acting oddly. I just didn't connect his behavior with his dad's behavior. He kept coming home later and later. I didn't like or approve of his two best friends who were using Kevin to shoplift clothing.

As the kids earned their driver's licenses, they drove the Monte Carlo. I took a dim view of this, so I decided I had to get back in the car and drive myself.

The challenge of driving was a big one, but I worked hard to conquer the problems and difficulties. Getting in and out of the car was an ordeal. I had to shift from the wheelchair into the car seat and then lift the wheelchair and put it in the car.

Although I had taken the driving course at Rancho Los Amigos back in California, I didn't have much experience operating a car with hand gears. Naturally it took me a while to switch my reflexes to my hands. I had to remember to push forward to stop and down to go. I practiced long and hard so I could pass the test to get my hand gear license, a feat I successfully accomplished.

Because I had been an avid driver and was enthusiastic to learn to drive again, it didn't take me very long to feel comfortable behind the wheel. I certainly had a greater appreciation for car mirrors than I ever had before.

Eventually, the kids' rough driving pretty much killed the Monte Carlo, forcing me to buy a new used car: a black 1971 El Camino with a camper top. It turned out to be the perfect car for me at the time. It boasted a 350-horsepower engine with good "get-up and go."

Each summer I'd pack the kids and my medical supplies into the El Camino and drive down to California for two or three weeks. Since I was living solely on Social Security disability benefits, my mom gave me money for the trips.

The drive from Oregon to California and back was extra challenging. Long drives bothered my back and shoulders. Since my balance had been affected by the damage from the bullet, sitting up for long periods of time took tremendous effort. My neck would get sore just holding my head up in the proper position to drive.

Nonetheless, these trips with the children were special to me because I dearly loved the closeness of traveling together.

My being in a wheelchair never really interfered, and memories of our trips are some of my most treasured.

We would stay at my parents' home during our trips to California. At first I was hopeful that Dad would be impressed that I had learned to drive again and he would appreciate my progress. But my fantasy didn't come to pass; he showed no interest whatsoever, acting as cold and distant as he'd always been. So, we would stay only until my dad became intolerable to the point where I couldn't take it anymore.

In fact, "cold and distant" was more positive than the tongue lashing he gave me when my wheelchair left indentations in the living room carpet. I was aghast.

Was he really complaining to me about the marks left by my wheelchair?

Could it be true?

I was crushed.

Here I was, obviously recovering well, raising the children and even driving, but he was enraged because my wheelchair temporarily marred his precious carpet.

While growing up, my sister Charlene and I would have earnest discussions about whether Dad was normal. When we spent the night at friends' houses, we observed other parents sitting and watching television with us or playing cards. Our dad would never dream of getting involved in any way with Charlene and I and our friends.

If Charlene and I wanted to watch TV with him, we'd have to watch what he was watching. We had to sit still and keep our mouths shut until the end of the show. We sat through programs that held no interest for us in an attempt to make him happy or see him smile. Sometimes we even made fudge or popcorn at night, but he'd never say so much as a thank you.

Charlene and I concluded that our father hated children. It made me wish he'd had four boys. I figured such a turn of events would probably have killed him!

One summer while I was visiting, I was startled to see Dad outside in the front yard picking up leaves while wearing his pajamas over his regular clothes.

"Mom, someone's going to throw a net over him," I said to my mother in alarm. "Can't you talk to him and straighten him out?"

"He's changed," Mom said. "I'm scared he might hit me."

It was the first-time Mom admitted something was wrong with him and that she was scared to try to talk to him. He had always been verbally abusive to her, taking on the role of a dictator, but he never raised a hand against her. Now she feared he would back up his angry words with physical violence.

I was now facing a different challenge with my father: he began acting in a strange way, even for him. Friends and family chalked it up to senility.

In the meantime, life progressed in Oregon. As the kids grew older they first worked in the berry fields, and Kim worked in the local grocery store.

Bill Johnson continued to be a big part of our family's life. Kim and Bill had been close since the minute we arrived in Scotts Mills, and their relationship evolved from friendship to love. Kim graduated from high school in 1978. The next year she discovered she was pregnant with Bill's baby.

My parents came to visit us at the same time Kim found out she was pregnant. Kim told her grandparents the news directly by announcing she was going to have a baby.

"I thought you were a good girl!" her grandfather yelled, slamming his fist on the table. Kim ran to Bill's house where she felt unconditionally loved by Bill and his family.

CHAPTER 17

Finding A Spiritual Community

The year after we moved to Scotts Mills, nine-year-old Paul was the catalyst for getting me to church. I'd been thinking about the possibility when one day Paul marched in and announced there was the "neatest church across the street." He invited me to come to church with him that very night.

I discovered the Scotts Mills Friends Church was down the hill from our house. It was within walking distance for us and it had a congregation of less than six dozen people. Sunday services were held in the grange hall. Of course, I couldn't make it there on my own since the hill was too steep for me to navigate in my wheelchair.

"They have services in the mornings and in the evenings so there's no way for you to back out!" he stated.

"Out of the mouths of babes," I thought and readily agreed.

It wasn't long until Paul and I showed up Sunday mornings and evenings, as well as for Bible study on Thursday night. We were the first of our family to attend on a regular basis and after a year the minister announced a toy drive.

The minister's request for donated toys was the catalyst for the entire family to clean out their closets and drawers and give away their excess toys. The night of the toy collection, the whole family showed up at church. Kim, Kevin and Kari were "checking it out" to make sure their mother and brother were doing the right thing. By this time Kim had given birth to her first child, Tiffany.

I was sitting in church with the family, praying, when one-year-old Tiffany came into the room carrying a pink princess telephone. It was the same pink princess phone I had used to call the prayer ministry.

Tiffany ran right up to me and deposited the princess phone into my lap. Of course, Tiffany had no idea how much that phone meant to me. Everyone noticed that Tiffany brought the phone to me, and of course they all knew

its special history. They were amazed. To me it was con-
firmation that this church was where I was meant to be, at
least for the time being. It was another divine sign that we
were in the right place.

Eventually I ended up joining the little nondenomina-
tional church. Although the entire family started attending church, Paul was the only one who loved going to that
church as much as I did. I was certain he was destined to
become a minister because he was so interested in being
there. Paul was very "church going and it was all him!" No
one ever had to suggest he get up to go to church. He made
sure he went to bed early on Saturday night so he could get
up on time for Sunday morning service.

I decided to be baptized in that church. All the partic-
ipants met on the banks of the river that had an Indian
name I can't recall. The Native American influence is evident everywhere. The area roads, cities, and rivers have
Indian names and I imagined how Indians had camped out
along the river.

Since the baptism occurred in the dead of winter; it was
freezing outside. The group gathered by a frozen waterfall.
I couldn't believe I was going to have to get baptized in the
frigid water. Nevertheless, everyone held his or her Bible

while the minister read a passage to celebrate each person who wanted to be baptized.

All the children except Kevin lined up to be baptized as well. The ice floating on the water was less than inviting. Each family member hoped and prayed that their dunking would be as quick as possible. One by one each child hurried into the water, and then burst out quickly, taking refuge in the car. I could not take the wheelchair into the river so two men carried me, dunked me, and brought me out again. As soon as we were all baptized, we headed home for a change of clothing before the fabric turned to ice. The experience warmed our hearts despite our frigid exteriors.

Becoming born again hit me so hard that it's all I talked about, all I felt, and all I thought about. Naturally I shared my excitement with my extended family, but they thought I'd somehow become a "Jesus freak."

I always appreciated the support I received from my fellow church-goers and often benefited from the prayers they offered on my behalf. One day people prayed for healing of my sores and colitis. I could have kept the congregants there for hours if I listed more of my medical problems. But the moment was so good and prayers for those two issues were enough.

I agree with the Christian teaching that forgiveness is very important. It's everything. If you don't forgive, you just close your mind to people. I would be a bitter old hag if I hadn't forgiven my dad for his harshness and Ron for abandoning me.

My belief in God keeps me going. To keep going doesn't take a lot of physical energy, but it does take a lot of mental energy and emotional calmness.

The only place my inspiration comes from is God. I pray a lot, but I also cry a lot. I'm human, and often I am awash in tears, asking for relief from my suffering. And sometimes I think God doesn't hear me.

I was blessed to have my granddaughter around.

I laughed when Tiffany went into the kitchen drawers and dragged out all of the Tupperware lids by herself. She'd sometimes sit inside the drawer and play with things one at a time. Tiffany especially loved playing with the pink princess phone in my bedroom, the phone I had used to call the prayer ministry after "The Voice" saved me from committing suicide.

I called my ex-husband Wayne to give him baby updates and to share my joy and excitement. I didn't think about our being divorced, but rather what a blessing it was that this new life had entered our world.

When Bill was seventeen and Kim was twenty, they married and moved out to live on their own. They stayed in the area. Bill had always seemed much older than his years, not just to Kim but to all who knew him. Tiffany was to be the first of three children from this union and each one of them were beautiful.

By now I had lived in Scott's Mills for four years. The church and the church community had played a big role in my life up until this point, but now I was forced to attend less and less because of a string of surgeries that confined me to bed.

At my doctor's suggestion, I had a bladder implant. The device they implanted was invented originally for men who were impotent. It enabled those men to achieve an erection by pressing a bulb implanted in their scrotum. In my case, the device was implanted on the outer labia. I would squeeze a pump that released sterile water from around a bladder net, allowing me to urinate. When it closed, it prevented leakage, giving me much more peace of mind when out in public. Before the implant, I continuously worried about public embarrassment.

As a result of the surgery, I was in an Oregon hospital for three long months. I called my mother frequently. Naturally I mentioned how sick I was and what I was going through. Unbeknownst to me, my mother called my dear friend Judy's parents to report on my condition and to let them know I was in the hospital without a reprieve in sight.

I was lying on the hospital's Clinitron bed when a little Easter Bunny puppet suddenly popped up on my shoulder. I looked up and was amazed to see my beloved friend Judy standing there sporting her hand puppet and grinning broadly.

We had been grade-school friends living only two doors away from each other. Later, Judy went on to Catholic school and I went to public school, but even though we were no longer at the same school, we remained dear friends. We were thick as thieves and played together every single day. Our friendship suffered when Judy's family moved to Northern California and we didn't get to see each other for years.

So this surprise visit was a treasure to me. She even hung a great big Easter Bunny on the front of my hospital door. Judy's visit lasted an entire week. We just had the best time; every day was a ball!

My hospital room boasted a lounge chair that went back all the way and converted into a makeshift bed. Judy slept there every night and didn't leave my side. The hospital staff turned a blind eye to the "visitor infraction," recognizing that this was the best possible therapy for me. And it was.

While I was still in the hospital, our family dogs were caught without their tags, and I received a ticket in the mail. However, the kids didn't let me know the ticket had come and when I got home from the hospital there was a warrant for my arrest.

I felt a warrant because of my dogs was ridiculous, so I called my local senator, Senator Hatfield. When I arrived at the courthouse I discovered there was no handicapped ramp, just stairs! This had to change and I told the senator that as well.

I pushed the issues until they finally put in a wheelchair ramp.

CHAPTER 18

Spiritual Conflicts

When I got home from the hospital, the kids told members of the church congregation that I could benefit from some help. As a result, a number of people came over to clean my kitchen and to help both me and the kids. I very much appreciated their help. But just as each person's life changes continually, so did the make-up and direction of the church.

The church elders, after much discussion, voted on some pivotal issues, the outcome of which changed the priorities and policies of the church. In addition, the elders argued publicly over who would hold the highest rank in the church hierarchy.

The battle of ego versus ego over who would be top dog had a negative effect on church members. The situation reminded me too much of the egotistical men I had known, so I became less and less interested in being involved in the church.

It really offended me that the arguments took place at church. I just could not feel good about anger, hostility, hurt feelings, and jealousy being aired in church. It felt most unchurch like!

"Paul, I just don't feel right at church any more. Have you noticed a change? How do you feel?"

"No, Mom, I'm not comfortable there any more either. It's just not the same."

To make things worse, I was completely dismayed about the judgmental statements and attitudes that members of the congregation leveled at me. They told me they didn't feel I had the "full word" in me because if I prayed harder and truly gave myself to the Lord, I'd be able to walk.

These "you're not doing it right which makes you a flawed Christian" comments wounded me deeply. These people knew nothing about what spiritual purpose this shooting had served and continued to serve in my life. They also knew nothing about spinal cord injuries. But they were good at making me feel like I somehow failed the course in the Christianity to which they ascribed.

I shared these comments with my doctor, who said it was just their ignorance speaking and they didn't know what they were talking about nor how their comments were hurting me. He suggested I tell them.

When I shared my feelings, many took offense despite the fact that I tried sincerely and nicely to explain where I was coming from.

"Yes, but all things are possible through God," I was told. I agreed, but I also pointed out that it was about God's will, not my will.

"If God wants it to be this way, and obviously He does, then I accept that," I explained. Try as I might, I could not get them to understand that there was a spiritual purpose behind what I was going through and that God put me where I was for a reason.

Every once in a while I would go back to church when I needed a lift, because no matter what it was still the Lord's House and a sacred place to me. That little church served a big purpose in our lives and as I say, most of my "Christian learning," which came from the Scotts Mills Friends Church, was of great value. But my disenchantment with the acrimony and my escalating medical problems kept me home most of the time.

I taught other people what it was like to live in a wheelchair because they didn't understand.

I took the kids to the mall to go shopping for school clothes. As I was making my way to the handicapped parking spot, a car pulled into it before I could. A woman and her daughter opened their doors, got out, and walked into the mall. I was enraged that someone would be that insensitive. I'd seen it before, but this time I was going to do something about it.

I pulled my car in behind that woman's car and parked.

I told the kids that we were waiting there until the lady came back.

The wait was long but finally she came out.

"Move your car out of my way," the lady ordered.

"No," I calmly said. "You are going to wait as long as I had to wait for you to get out of the mall."

The lady didn't know what to say.

"And," I started. "You are going to watch and see what it takes for me to get out of my car and what my children have to deal with so you can understand why these parking spaces are designed especially for people in wheelchairs."

I proceeded to unfold my legs from the car, swivel in the seat then grab the wheelchair from behind the seat. I didn't rush with this; I wanted her to see that just getting out of the car was a struggle.

When I finished, I looked at the lady and she was crying. "Thank you," she said and apologized to me.

CHAPTER 19

Kids Moving Out

I first started going to Alcoholics Anonymous in 1974 when I lived in Southern California. The spiritual aspect of the program was extremely meaningful to me. I watched self-confessed alcoholics, former atheists, and agnostics express their feelings about God and become sober men and woman. I was truly elated at the progress I witnessed. I saw them bring their families into AA to "get the message." I observed miracle transformations.

Now that my church no longer served me, I turned to AA once again. Unfortunately, no AA meetings were held in Scotts Mills and the closest meetings were in Salem, an hour away. This distance proved problematic since I wasn't driving much anymore and I couldn't find anyone who was willing to pick me up and take me to and from meetings. There were a couple of men who volunteered, but rather than being altruistic, they ended up trying to grope me and take advantage of me. Nevertheless, by hook or by crook, or by groper, I found my way to meetings. I love AA because it brings me closer to God.

Kari moved out of the house when she turned eighteen and moved back to Southern California. At first she went to the San Diego area and lived with my sister Charlene for a while. Then she moved in with her future husband, David, who was a grocery clerk. The two worked very hard to make ends meet.

Kari confided in me that in a way she was glad I had been shot because it gave her more time with me. I understood. In a sense, I grew up right along with Kari and the other children because I was starting life over again, this time from the perspective of being paralyzed and in a wheelchair. I went through all the stages—from infancy to adulthood—as a paraplegic, and in the process bonded strongly with my children.

My father's condition worsened and he mercifully died in 1985. Later they discovered he had Alzheimer's, which explained his bizarre and erratic behavior.

Because of my spiritual work with the Lord, I had worked through many of the issues and was able to forgive him fully. I had lost the rancor and hatred, and could love him. Coming all that way undoubtedly was one of my biggest life lessons for which I achieved an A+. Even so, I could not shed a tear, nor did I go see him at the funeral parlor. I just couldn't. My inability to cry and my lack of grief overwhelmed me.

When Paul turned eighteen, I told him he now could change his last name to Riddle with no problem whatsoever. But Paul didn't have any inclination to do so. He liked having the same last name, Magness, as his brother and sisters, and at the time, pretty much hated Ron for what he "thought" Ron did to his mother.

By the time they were eight or nine, I had informed all the children about Paul's true biological father. The information was immaterial to all of them. Paul was their brother, period. Nothing could change or diminish their love and acceptance of him.

Later that same year Paul moved out of the house and moved back to California. He left to go work for my nephew who owned a home remodeling business. The move was fortuitous for both Paul and his cousin.

Kevin had been in and out of institutions so much, it was as though he had already left home.

Scotts Mills has a yearly event called Summer Fest that they hold in the park. The day after the festival in 1986 I took my car out to see how well it performed after having some repairs. Since seat belts were not mandated by law, I didn't buckle up.

I left the house and turned left and headed downhill on Grandview. Road crews used gravel in the winter to give cars traction in the ice and snow, but this year's rain had washed the gravel down to one spot in the road, accumulating in a pile of gravel near the bottom of the hill. I hit the gravel, jolting me and the car. As I approached the intersection, I started pumping the hand brake. The brakes didn't respond.

I couldn't figure out for the life of me why.

All I knew is that I was careening downhill, the car would not slow down, and it wouldn't stop. I started to panic as I went flying toward the stop sign at the bottom of the hill.

Somehow, I managed to turn right onto Fourth Avenue where it met up with Crooked Finger Road. I hit a dip at this junction, catapulting my car into the air. I flew across

Crooked Finger and went off a small cliff, smashing into some Douglas Fir trees and landed on a boulder. I was thrown onto the floor on the passenger side of the vehicle. A tree fell on top of the car. Then everything stopped. I couldn't move to free myself so I had to wait. The fire department arrived and they literally cut me out of the car. Once freed, the rescue squad took me to the hospital.

Once again I found myself in the emergency room of a hospital—not my favorite place to be. The attending physician informed me that I had suffered a broken neck but the surgeon, who would work on me most effectively, was out of town for two days. In the meantime, they put me in traction until the surgeon's return.

In the hospital I learned that when the car struck the boulder, the frame bent so severely that the doors couldn't be opened. That's why I had to be cut out. And I found out that my left foot was behind the brake pedal, making it impossible to apply the brakes. When I hit the gravel, the jolt must have caused my left foot to fall under the brake pedal. I was completely unaware that my booted foot, devoid of sensation thanks to the paralysis, was keeping the brake from being activated.

Once the surgeon arrived, he looked at the x-rays but declared he wanted a new set of his own to be taken. He supervised the x-ray session since he had specific ideas of what positions he felt would be most advantageous for an accurate diagnosis. It was critical for him to have the right view of my neck to know whether or not I would have to wear a crown, or what is sometimes called a halo. Such a device screws directly into the skull and rests on the person's shoulders in order to hold the neck perfectly in alignment. They are usually worn for a grueling six months.

After the X-rays the surgeon told me that my neck was healing so rapidly that he was going to leave me in traction for five days and then send me home with only a collar to wear. If I'd had some confetti, I would have thrown it in the air.

Since the accident happened in the middle of town on a weekend when so many people were in the park, it became common knowledge. It even made the papers, leaving me feeling humiliated by the publicity of the incident. I was embarrassed that anyone knew about the accident.

People teased me because Summer Fest featured beer and wine. Comments were made about me still being drunk from the night before. They were laughing, but I wasn't—

especially since I hadn't had a single drink the night before or on the day of the accident.

Once I was home I saw my El Camino. I was blown away by the extent of the damage. The car was literally bent in half and could not be repaired, and I was forced to buy a new car. It was quite some time before I could see the humor in the incident: the doctors were worried about me breaking my neck when I was already paralyzed!

I bought a 1972 El Camino—a faster version of the first car—and this new car boasted a 396-horsepower engine. Despite my previous harrowing experiences—such as rolling a car off the road, being run over by a trike, a three wheeled motorcycle, and this recent flying crash—I still loved fast cars and loved to drive them!

I realized that in some bizarre way, I was lucky. Most of the accidents—and there have been a lot of them—would have killed most people. Besides the car accidents, I'd survived attempted strangulations, and had been beaten up, and shot. Friends and relatives would kid me, saying "God doesn't want you yet!"

CHAPTER 20

Male Companionship

Ten years after we moved to Scotts Mills, Wayne and his third wife showed up at my front door without so much as a five-minute warning. Of course I was stunned to see Wayne standing in the doorway, but delighted he had come by to see the children. Although he and his wife lived in Oklahoma, they had come to Oregon on vacation. I had really liked his second wife, but this third one was a doozy. She was not at all pleased to see me.

Wayne and his wife relaxed, and as the visit became longer the conversation began to wander. We reminisced about the "good old days" and the genuinely good parts of our relationship. I showed Wayne a photo I cherished and which brought tears to my eyes. The photo was taken when

Kim was a toddler. Kim was sitting in the middle of a flattened cardboard box in which a new bed had been shipped. Wayne was dragging her around the back yard, giving her a ride just as the sun was going down and Kim was laughing. It was sweet to remember that there had been genuinely good times, and the photo was an eloquent testament to them.

At one point, I brought up our divorce. I wanted to explain that I hadn't tried to take the children away from him and that I had been willing to compromise about everything. I questioned him as to why he never mentioned the divorce to me in any of our phone conversations or even now. When the subject of the official divorce papers came up, Wayne shocked me by admitting he had never signed the official papers and had failed to send them in to be legally filed.

Suddenly it dawned on me that he and I had never been officially divorced.

I was aghast at this revelation; twenty-seven years had passed and we were still legally married! Wayne kind of shrugged it all off and focused on other subjects, although he did promise to "take care of it." The visit ended on a friendly note as we bid each other goodbye.

Chapter 20

Several months later, my phone rang at seven o'clock in the morning. I was shocked and most unhappy to hear it was a lawyer who was representing the third Mrs. Magness. He informed me that I was being sued for divorce and for half of everything that I currently owned.

It turned out that when Wayne's third wife heard that Wayne was in fact a bigamist and was still married to me, she plotted to take advantage of the situation by suing me to get everything she could. I did not take the news lying down!

I consulted with the local District Attorney in Oregon. He calculated that Wayne owed me at least $149,000 in back child support payments which I could collect by mandating a court review of every one of his income tax statements.

"Listen here, sister," I said emphatically when I reached Wayne's wife on the phone, "It cost us two thousand dollars to move into that house in Orange County and we only lived in that house together for two years. I was there for a total of twelve additional years so I hardly think I owe Wayne half of twelve years of payments! I received no child support from Wayne over all those years. If you take me to court, I will slam you with back child support orders like you've never dreamt of in your worst nightmare!"

I told the current Mrs. Magness that she'd better stop the whole process. By that time, the papers had been signed and filed. At last Wayne and I were legally divorced.

"That's all there is to it now," I stressed to the woman. "Leave me and my kids alone and stay out of our lives."

I never heard any more about it. I was certain the lawyer had told Wayne's wife that the back child support payments could and would be mandated so she'd be far better off letting sleeping dogs lie.

Ron and I still spoke on the phone occasionally. During one recent conversation, two years after telling off the third Mrs. Magness, we decided to get together.

Because Kim still hated Ron so much and blamed him for my injuries, I decided it was prudent not to mention my decision to see him. This decision added a somewhat clandestine flavor to our reunion.

Ron and I agreed to meet in a little town in Oregon called Pendleton. We chose that location for two reasons: it was a day's travel for each of us so it was like meeting in the middle, and Pendleton was the location of the penitentiary in which Kevin was incarcerated. This way I could visit my son as well as Ron, who was still my legal husband.

I arranged for a friend of Paul's to drive me to a Pendleton motel that Ron and I had chosen for our get-together. After twelve long years, my nerves got the best of me when the time came to reunite with Ron. I had to admit to myself that I was filled with anxiety.

Would he still be attracted to me? Would my colostomy bag turn him off? Would he be able to handle my disability? How would he treat me? What would he look like? A thousand questions plagued me.

I painstakingly put on my makeup and did my hair in my favorite, and hopefully most attractive style. I got all dressed up to impress Ron and make him happy to see me.

I arrived at the motel around eleven in the evening as nervous as I was, my concerns evaporated almost immediately. As we pulled up to the motel, Ron was standing outside waiting for me. For a moment I was shocked at how much older he looked and how much his appearance had changed. He was clad in familiar attire—Levi's and a shirt—but his body builder physique had disappeared. My brain took in this information, but my heart opened as my love for Ron rekindled on the spot.

Ron ran to the car, flung open the door, and hugged me enthusiastically.

We clung to each other for several minutes and then Ron helped me into my wheelchair. Then we hugged some more. Once inside the motel room, I asked Ron to help me onto the bed so I could sit next to him.

Like the old, dear friends that we were, we sat side by side talking animatedly and glancing at the television between torrents of words. A baseball game was being aired and since Ron was a baseball freak, he was eager to share his passion for the game with me. He regaled me with inside information about the players and quoted a barrage of statistics sharing his excitement and considerable knowledge. I enjoyed hearing the trivia and his stories of baseball legends that made his eyes light up.

I was amazed at how my old feelings for Ron came flooding back almost immediately. And the rush of returned feelings was mutual. Before long, our hugs evolved into passion. Love making was a natural result. Although I could no longer have an orgasm due to my paralysis, the closeness of our physical union gave me a great deal of pleasure and satisfaction. I was back in the arms of the man

I had never stopped loving and who was still my lawfully wedded husband. I felt great!

We spent twenty-four glorious, precious hours together in that motel room. We had pizza delivered and didn't leave the room. Between the animated conversations, love making, and baseball, we updated each other on our lives and found out what each had been up to.

Truth is that I had not expected to feel this strong resurgence of love for Ron. Since we had been physically separated for more than a decade, I really hadn't known what to expect.

Amazingly, I was not angry with him for abandoning me. I put myself in Ron's shoes, and in an intellectual way, I understood that he couldn't handle the situation. Of course, I had been broken hearted when he left me, but because he was drinking so heavily, I recognized that his leaving was a good thing.

I simply could not have handled him under those trying circumstances. In addition, the move to Oregon resulted in part from Ron leaving, and the children and I became closer than ever because of that move. There was a higher purpose to things having happened the way they did.

Parting the next morning at eleven was painful, but we vowed to stay in touch and see each other more often. After that, my long-distance telephone bills reflected our frequent conversations.

For the first ten years that I lived in Scotts Mills, I pretty much stayed home. I had partied with neighbors and noticed how much they drank. People were always going to bars both in Scotts Mills and to the Markum Inn in Marquam, the next town over. Although the population of each town was only two hundred, each town was served by at least two or three bars.

For several years, while I could still drive, I would go to the Markum Inn on the weekends. The Inn and the gas station on the opposite corner served as the heart of Markquam. In fact, the Inn and the gas station accounted for the entire downtown.

Since the area had no major highways or anything that remotely resembled a highway, drivers had to deal with back country roads to get to the Inn. Despite the winding roads, people came from all over the area to dine at the Markum Inn and it was inundated every Friday, Saturday, and Sunday.

Benches rimmed the perimeter of the Inn so people could sit while they waited, sometimes for hours, to gain entry. The Markum Inn was the spot where everybody in the area gravitated. Every time I showed up, I saw people I knew and I'd have a good time visiting with them.

At first I tried to party with the best of them, but soon discovered that my stomach could no longer tolerate excessive alcohol. I would be sick for days after drinking and quickly decided I didn't like the pay-off. Yet I was terribly lonely and yearned for companionship.

From time to time, I would meet someone interesting whom I would decide to date. Mostly my dates were with younger men since most men my age tended to date younger women.

Once I accepted an invitation from a man from the church. He took me out for dinner and right then and there he asked if I was able to have sex. What an impertinent question! He was rude and absurd to ask such a thing so prematurely in the relationship, and his actions ticked me off.

Without question, dating was very different since my wheelchair was in the picture. My dates would have to put the chair in the trunk, often making the date awkward.

Half the time I would drive myself rather than be picked up, so I could avoid any unpleasant "surprises" in my date's car and go home whenever I wanted.

One man didn't seem to mind the wheelchair or my paralysis at all. I called him "Leo the Russian." Leo had been born in the U.S., but his parents were Russian and Turkish born and had lived in Russian villages. That's where his nickname came from. Leo was eleven years younger than me.

I met Leo in a restaurant in the town of Woodburn, seven miles from Scotts Mills. Not surprisingly, considering my past, Leo drank too much. My pattern of choosing men who drank and did drugs excessively remained unblemished.

I quickly became aware that Leo had problems at home so I provided an understanding ear for him. We would talk endlessly whenever we were together.

Leo brought a big dose of fun into my life. He loved to take me places where I would normally not have been able to go. Leo learned that when he focused on tending to someone else's needs, his own problems receded. We enjoyed boating, fishing, digging for relics, and playing in the snow. Relics abounded in the area, and on our outings we'd find ancient shells, bones, and tools. We also loved driving up into the country to go as far as we could get into the thick timber. We enjoyed frequent drives along the rivers, stopping to have lunch while taking in the beautiful scenery.

We'd often drive two-and-a-half hours to the Oregon coast. I relished such outings. The mountains were much more accessible than the coast, so in fifteen minutes we could be playing in the snow. Leo would pick me up out of the passenger seat of his car and throw me in the snow. We laughed and romped like teenagers.

However, Leo was bedeviled by booze and drugs. Although I clung to denial because I so enjoyed the fun we had together, the relationship finally wore out after six years. There was no big ugly break-up, but rather just a gradual attrition.

CHAPTER 21

Truly On My Own

Kim, Bill, and their three children lived close by. But after ten years of marriage Bill was in an auto accident and died. In the car with him was a woman with whom he was having an affair.

Ten-year-old Tiffany took his death the hardest. She cried all the time and came to me continually for solace and an explanation of the unexplainable. It would be five years before family members could mention his name in front of her without her falling apart.

Kim, too, was upset when Bill died. She reeled from the knowledge that he was having yet another affair—he had had several—but in the end, she hated losing him. Truth was the entire family loved Bill. He had his flaws, but he was such a wonderful person that everyone adored his company.

I kept in monthly contact with Ron via telephone. I was always glad to hear from him since I had no ill will towards him whatsoever. We'd catch up with each other and share what was happening in our respective lives. Over the years, Ron had lived in Las Vegas and then in Idaho where he worked in a mine for a decade. Eventually he moved back to Vegas. Other than our one visit, I had not seen Ron again.

Ron tried to surprise me by showing up at our door in Scotts Mills but, I wasn't there.

Never once during our monthly phone conversations, did Ron bring up the accident, and throughout the years, Ron continued to drink despite suffering two cataclysmic episodes like the one that occurred when he went to AA with me back in Garden Grove. His addiction and his guilt drove him to the brink of self-destruction.

As the children grew up and came of age, they moved away one by one, and I was alone in the house.

I took in roommates to help with the bills and the upkeep of the house. However, I did not care for the way in which the roommates treated the house and soon grew weary of the arrangement. The constant presence of roommates eroded my privacy. To have a little alone time, I would drive myself down to the park, take the T-roof off the new Firebird my mom had helped me buy, and bask in the sun. Driving that car around the area made me as happy as could be. But one day, having a roommate paid off in spades.

One morning I was preparing the Easter ham. I was eager to get the food preparation out of the way so I could shower and get dressed. I placed the ham in a baking pan and used a towel to hold the pan as I put it into the hot oven. Without realizing it, the towel touched the oven's electric element and caught on fire. Unknowingly, I put the flaming towel down in my lap and the fire spread quickly to my knee socks. Because I was paralyzed with no feeling in my legs, I didn't feel any heat or burning sensation.

My roommate happened to glance into the kitchen and saw what was happening. She dashed in and put out the fire by throwing a towel over my legs and starving the flames of oxygen. That was one day I was extremely grateful for a roommate!

I had a Clinitron bed. This unique bed is oval-shaped and has a nylon-covered mattresses filled with tiny granules or beads that look like fine white sand. When the motor is turned on, air is pumped in and the granules turn to an almost fluid state. Lying on the bed feels literally like floating on air.

The mattress feels like a waterbed, only a little firmer. It is a boon for people like me who suffer from sores and wounds. It releases all pressure from any point on the body. I discovered that I could lie on the bed for days at a time without moving and, unlike conventional mattresses, it wouldn't cause any problems. The Clinitron was developed for stroke patients and for surgical patients who simply could not be moved at all, but it turned out to have a much broader application for other conditions.

These benefits come with a cost. The pumps emit a loud throbbing sound as the air is pumped in. By setting the dial a certain way, air is released in part of the mattress to create an automatic roll-over from left to right while I lay on it. Every one hundred and twenty minutes the air is slowly expelled on one side and filled on the other. The process is so slow that I am barely aware of the shift, but nonetheless it turns me from my left side to flat on my back and then to my right side and back again. The only telltale sign I notice is in my neck: my head gets displaced from its position on the pillow and sometimes I end up in an awkward position.

I often awake in the middle of the night and shove my pillows around to ensure a comfortable sleep.

The bed was hard to sleep on and I wasn't the only one who hated it. My roommates took a dim view of the Clinitron bed because it was constantly throbbing and making loud buzzing sounds as it rolled me over.

By 1990, I grew weary of having both the roommates and the responsibility of the house. Kim and I decided that Kim and her three children would move into the house while I would move into my own apartment. I was still dating Leo at the time and was looking forward to some privacy.

I rented an apartment on Water Street in Silverton. The heavy responsibility of taking care of the house was now a thing of the past, much to my relief. Besides, I figured it was better for Kim and the children to enjoy the house. My apartment was only a seven-minute drive to the house, so it wasn't like I was moving to the other side of the moon.

I was incredibly happy in my new little apartment. I felt a sense of independence that I hadn't experienced for a very long time. I lived there four years and was still dating Leo. I devised ways to get myself around to do most of the things I wanted to do. I got out the door in my wheelchair even when snow had fallen. I laughed as I slid to the car, euphoric with the realization that "I can do it myself." However, the "I can" attitude could not prevent accidents from happening.

One day I was transferring myself from my car to my wheelchair and I engaged the brakes completely on the wheelchair wheels. Yet, the wheelchair slid out from under me when I scooted out of the car seat. I fell out of the car and hit my posterior on the doorjamb. I did manage to pull myself up because my arms were strong. I developed a sore on my backside, and that required a lot of doctoring and attention. I discovered that sores in paralyzed people don't heal quickly because of the lack of movement and blood flow, and the sores can become a real problem.

I learned that Ron had stopped drinking, but after he took his last drink he suffered a series of six convulsions. I was convinced that Ron's body, after not having a drink for twenty-four hours, went into shock which started the first of the series of convulsions. I heard this is a very common response for those who drink tremendous quantities of alcohol on a daily basis.

Of course, it would have been suicide for Ron to continue drinking.

He nearly died from alcohol poisoning and had to have his esophagus rebuilt. The surgery was painful, naturally, and once he went through that process he simply could not drink any more.

Eighteen years after I was shot, Paul married. When I went to the wedding I was amazed that Ron showed up. I thought: How could he do this? How could he come and face me at our child's wedding when he hasn't wanted to be a part of our lives before? I've only seen him once since 1975. We have talked often but that was with me and not with Paul. He'd had little contact with Paul as far as I knew.

I reeled with the memory of how I felt when I came out of rehab to discover how heavily Ron was drinking. I wondered how could he have asked me to tolerate him in that drunken state and take care of four kids. At the time, I didn't know how I could handle it. All I could do was hang on to my children as tightly as possible so I could be next to them and be with them. The one thing God gave me that I can never be ungrateful for is my children!

As I came back to the present and looked at Ron sitting there at Paul's wedding, I had to admit that Ron didn't seem to have the same strong feelings for his children that I had for mine.

I thought back to the years that stretched between the accident and Paul's wedding. As far as I knew, Ron had not seen any of his children from his first marriage to Beverly and his contact with Paul was minimal too.

I also admitted, both to Ron and to myself, that it bothered me that he had not helped me out financially. I once asked him why he didn't help me out financially.

"I don't make enough money," he said.

Ron's response was less than satisfying to me. I couldn't work because of my injuries. I lived alone in a wheelchair and raised four kids, without a job and, he tells me he has no money?

I challenged him. "What do you do with yourself? Go to bars?"

Ron swore he didn't frequent bars any more, but that didn't change the fact that he didn't feel he could send me money. Just like he couldn't be with me because the wheelchair reminded him of what he did to me.

CHAPTER 22

The End of Independence

I relied heavily on my arms and shoulders to maneuver myself around. I had always been a petite woman. I was a cheerleader in high school and my weight had been between ninety-eight pounds and one hundred and twenty-five pounds most of my life. However, my shoulders and arms bore the brunt of every move.

I didn't baby myself or my shoulders. I moved furniture around so I could vacuum behind it. I washed and waxed floors, and cleaned the carpet. Whatever the task, if it was remotely within my ability to accomplish it, I did it. My arms enabled me to shift me from the wheelchair to bed and back out again. I never gave a thought to easing up on my shoulders. They served as my workhorses once my legs could no longer carry me.

I suffered chronic pain in my shoulders but resigned myself that such discomfort went with the territory. My physician gave me a shot of cortisone every other month for two years to cloak the pain and keep me going. I accepted it as standard operating procedure.

One night, a girlfriend and I stopped at a restaurant in Mt. Angel that was hosting Taco Night. I was pushing myself out of the car and into the wheelchair seat when fire ripped through my left shoulder. Of course, it wasn't really fire, but it sure felt like it.

Despite the pain, my friend grabbed the back of my pants and I got into the chair. We went inside, but didn't stay long because I was in so much pain.

We left the restaurant and drove the few minutes back to my apartment in Silverton. My friend helped me get inside and undressed, and put me to bed before leaving for the night.

I woke up in excruciating pain, and I couldn't move anything on my left side. I called Kevin and my boyfriend Leo, who came immediately to take me to a doctor. The doctor quickly referred me to a specialist, who informed me that I had torn my rotator cuff. I required surgery. Nothing else would work, he emphasized, yet he could not guarantee the success of the surgery.

He said the aftermath of the surgery would be painful and difficult. I'd already suffered through a series of surgeries so I figured I could handle yet another one.

Recovery from shoulder surgery proved to be painful indeed, as well as extremely difficult, but I was up to the challenge. I endured the cast for three months, gamely performing the exercises prescribed by my doctor and physical therapist. When all was said and done, my recovered shoulder seemed to be in good working order.

Two months after my recovery, I took a short drive by myself. When I returned home, I eased out of the car and felt a familiar, horrifying pain sear through my right arm and shoulder. I knew immediately I had damaged my right shoulder in the exact same way as the left shoulder had been injured.

Luckily my neighbor John was outside, so he ran to my aid when I cried out for help. John showered me with kindness and care. I began to cry; the reality of what lay before me loomed clearly in my mind. I was going to have to repeat the shoulder surgery for the other side.

I returned to the doctor who had operated on my left shoulder. The thought of yet another surgery and recovery filled me with anguish. Yet I could see no other course of action.

The second surgery was performed, but this time while I was in a cast I began experiencing significant pain in my left shoulder—the shoulder that had been operated on first. Could it be the surgery had reversed itself?

My worst fears were confirmed: despite the surgeries, I would never regain the use of my shoulders. I believe to this day that the real damage was done by too many cortisone shots in my shoulders. Cortisone can cause osteoporosis and erode bone and cartilage. As a result, I could no longer scoot myself anywhere, let alone from bed to wheelchair and back. Nineteen years from the time I first learned how to take care of myself in rehab, I was now unable to take care of myself. I had to give up my beloved driving along with all vestiges of independence.

In essence, I was bedridden.

Only my faith and hopefulness pulled me through this catastrophic turn in my life.

CHAPTER 23

Physical Trials

While living in Oregon, I had six surgeries due to my spinal cord injury. And for extra excitement, I had my gall bladder removed as well.

I was thrilled when I was given a new portable intravenous system that had recently been devised and was now being used at the hospital. This device enabled me to return home sooner. I called the portable IV "miraculous!" No longer did they have to send me home with a big, cumbersome IV system for the bed. Now the new system was comprised of a little computer box and a small container of antibiotics. The unit featured a timer that automatically dispensed the precise dosage of antibiotic at the right time.

The new device was really amazing, but even with that, at the age of fifty-one, almost twenty years from the day of the shooting, the loss of the use of my shoulders meant that my days of living alone were over.

My daughter Kari was in the process of divorcing her first husband David. They had separated and reconciled many times, but finally had to let the marriage go. She moved back to Southern California, and she asked me to come live with her and the kids. Kari pointed out that her training as a paramedic would enable her to take good care of me. Naturally, I was overwhelmed with depression over my physical condition, but was grateful for my daughter's kind offer.

I knew if I stayed in Oregon, my daughter Kim would have to take care of me. I couldn't bear for that to happen since Kim had already taken care of me for so many years and she just wasn't going to agree to it any longer. However, I didn't realize or consider what life would be like living with a single mom and her kids.

One of my aides was getting married and was going to Southern California at the same time I needed to go. The aide would drive my car with me inside while her family followed behind in their van. I was grateful for such ideal timing and my aide's valuable assistance.

I got help packing up my car with everything I could salvage from my life in Oregon. I said farewell to the apartment I had loved so much, my furniture, and a great many other material possessions. My life was being pared down to an even more basic level.

More devastating than the loss of my personal possessions was the loss of the close friends I had enjoyed during eighteen years of living in Oregon. Of course, I had friends and family back in Southern California, but they were all quite a distance from Kari's home in Oceanside. The drive to reach any of my friends was at least an hour one way, while my aunts and uncles lived about one hundred miles away.

It seemed impossible that my life could get any worse, but with these recent events it had deteriorated to the extreme. I put on a brave face to those around me, but no one knew that most of my alone time was spent in tears. Suicide never entered my consciousness, thanks to the Lord.

I was greatly cheered by moving in with Kari and by just being around her. Kari was upbeat and bright eyed, which made everything seem better. I remembered how energetic

Kari was and what a people-magnet she had always been. Nothing had changed. She still loved people and people loved her back.

Kari's sons Jeff, aged five, and Justin, aged two, had a difficult adjustment to my moving in with them. They hadn't grown up with me in a wheelchair like my other grandchildren had, and so they weren't used to being with me.

While I lived with Kari and my grandsons, Kari met Marine Gunnery Sergeant Kyle Garvin. I was delighted to see Kari happy and content. They would get married in a couple of years.

From the moment I arrived, Kari had no trouble whatsoever moving me around. As a paramedic, she was used to moving people of all sizes. My ninety-eight pounds was no heavier than a feather to Kari. I felt completely safe and confident in her loving care, whether she was moving me to the wheelchair, into the shower, or into the car. For this I was extremely grateful.

After I had settled in, Kari told me about an orthopedic specialist she had met who worked with the San Diego Chargers football players. Kari had asked him about my shoulders, so he suggested Kari bring me in so he could assess my condition to see what he could do. He was optimistic and willing to see me, even though I was on Medicare.

Kari was never going to give up and neither was I.

The doctor ordered x-rays along with several MRIs. The results were devastating: nothing could be done to restore my shoulders. He told us the only thing he could do was to put in a couple of artificial shoulders, yet these would not allow me to lift my body weight and move around the way I used to move around. He said the artificial shoulders would pop out of joint if I put any weight on them so I would be in and out of the doctor's office for adjustments all the time.

Kari and I had to admit this did not sound like a good option. The bottom line was I was stuck with my shoulders the way they were. My tendons were all stretched out. I fervently believed the series of cortisone shots was the cause of my shoulder deterioration.

Whatever the cause, the effect was the same: I was bed-ridden and helpless. I could no longer choose whether to stay in bed or get up. I had to wait for someone's assistance, which left me feeling completely helpless.

The bladder implant I had been given while living in Oregon had served me well for over a decade. But once I moved to Oceanside, the implant sprung a leak, wreaking havoc with my health.

The implant had to be removed. I later discovered that surgery in the pubic area, whether it is done on females or males, often results in blood clots. Two days after surgery to remove the implant, I developed blood clots in both my left leg and right lung.

Once the clots were detected, I received anticoagulants to dissolve the clots in my lung. Luckily, it did the trick and dissolved the clots before they did serious damage.

The next thing I knew, I was back in the operating room. Surgeons inserted a mesh basket in my leg to trap the clot and stop it from moving any higher. The clot in my lung had lodged high because movement propels blood clots further and further up the body. Since I could move my upper torso, the blood clot had traveled to my lung. But the blood clot in my leg had remained fairly stable since my legs were paralyzed. I obviously wasn't moving them around. This bought the doctors some time to insert the basket. The basket is still in my leg to this day.

The surgery was successful, but all the complications resulted in an extra-long stay in the hospital. Recovery from the blood clots and the basket surgery was compounded by another bout of pneumonia and blood poisoning all at once. The confluence of problems took a toll on me and impeded both my speech and my memory. My thought processes became foggy, and at times I didn't even know where I was. Once, I called Paul at three in the morning and asked him to come get me. I didn't realize the hospital was eighty miles away from Paul. All my mental processes were muddled.

When my other grandchildren were born, I was able to get into a car or get a ride to be at the hospital when they came out of the delivery room. I wept from my desire to do the same with Paul's babies. My dream was to get behind the steering wheel and drive the eighty miles to Paul's house when his first baby was born.

Of course I recognized what was involved for me to go to Paul's home for a weekend and that in the past, a weekend turned into a week because so much special equipment had to be hauled along with me. I had to bring all my personal care products—a suitcase with special bathing equipment and what had become my "regular hygiene stuff." The power mattress that I slept on had to be transported and then hooked up at the other end.

Realistically, how many times a month could I go for a visit? I'd be lucky to go once a month and it was a lot to put Paul through. I just couldn't do that to him. But I wanted to see Paul's face when he saw his beautiful child and be there the first time he held his baby. So I just had to drive down there myself!

When the time came, I was unable to drive myself, of course, but Pam, one of Kari's friends, made sure I got to see the baby the very next day after her birth. Despite the twenty-four-hour delay, I was delirious with joy to hold my new granddaughter!

I wanted to get this baby girl her first doll, just like I did with my granddaughter Tiffany. I wanted to get her a special doll, not just an ordinary one but a Raggedy Ann or Andy doll, something she would have all her life. I yearned for the normal experiences almost every grandmother in the world could count on having.

Unfortunately, my shoulders were not the only problem. For years I was plagued with pneumonia. My lungs were vulnerable due to scar tissue damage caused by the shooting. I was in and out of hospitals constantly with pneumonia and collapsed lungs—just one more difficulty that came with the territory.

With all the physical trials and tribulations I suffered, Kari was kept busy running me to doctors and hospitals. This responsibility weighed heavily on her, so she was very excited to discover the existence of a new service dubbed "Call Doc." Thanks to the energy and investment of Dr. John Winkler, Call Doc brought a physician right to our door.

I considered it a miracle that Dr. Winkler came into my life, driving a big van that carried an x-ray machine and dental equipment. I thought the service was utterly fabulous since no one had to take me to the doctor any more. Dr. Winkler serviced people who were bedridden, had suffered heart attacks, or who were paralyzed like me— anyone who had a difficult time getting up and out to a doctor's office.

I thought Dr. Winkler was extremely nice and was thrilled with Call Doc in every possible regard. Dr. Winkler had great empathy for me and the chronic pain caused by my shoulders. He prescribed morphine, which relieved much suffering.

He was an M.D. who practiced holistic medicine. Dr. Winkler recognized that conventional medicine didn't have all the answers, especially for chronic situations like mine. He suggested I take glucosamine and chondroitin supplements in an attempt to regrow shoulder tissue. When I began taking the supplements, I couldn't reach straight up in the air or behind me and I couldn't comb my hair or lift anything heavier than a quart of milk.

At first I didn't even notice that I was reaching for things that I couldn't have before, and was doing so without thinking about it. I'd been on the supplements only a month when my nurse observed I had a great deal more mobility than before.

"What do you think caused you to have greater mobility?" she asked.

At first I had no idea, but then it dawned on me: it must be the glucosamine and chondroitin. Suddenly I realized I could lift myself a little bit, reach behind me, brush my hair and put on makeup. I could just about bathe myself as well, although I still required help getting in and out of the shower chair.

Thanks to this improvement, my arms grew stronger and I was able to scoot myself off the bed into the wheelchair. I could even dress myself for the most part. I still needed help snapping my bra and putting on my pants. Putting on pants was always the hardest challenge of getting dressed because I had to lie down and reach behind me to pull the back of my pants up first. This process always hurt my shoulders so when I was done, I felt like I'd been through a real workout.

In 1996, my neighbor, who had worked in a nursing home, assured me she could safely transfer me from wheelchair to the shower chair and back for my daily shower. Both of us were confident in her ability to make the transfer after my daily shower. Out of necessity, my neighbor had removed the handle from the side of the wheelchair in order to get me out of and back into the chair. Even so, I took a tumble in the shower and fell to the floor. On my way down, I hit the end of the wheelchair where there was exposed tubing. This accident scraped off my skin completely, leaving a raw spot on my backside.

I developed a sore on my behind that eventually penetrated right down to the bone and was nearly catastrophic. Plastic surgery was necessary to put me back together again properly. To add insult to injury, I contracted pneumonia while I was in the hospital for treatment of the sore.

Throughout our regular phone contact, Ron frequently brought up my long-ago affair with Glenn. And now, five years after Paul's wedding, Ron was still bringing up ancient history, which infuriated me. After all, I reminded him, he had left me and we were separated at the time of my affair. I reasoned that it wasn't like I had cheated on him when we were together.

Nonetheless, Ron couldn't or wouldn't let go of it! I got so sick and tired of him throwing that at me. I loved him. He was my husband. I even forgave him for shooting me. What else could I do to prove that he was the only man I loved?

After all this time I was now no longer willing to get so upset and cry for hours after talking to him. This time my anger and hurt came out and I told him I didn't want to talk to him ever again.

CHAPTER 24

New State of Living

While living with Kari, I naturally became friends with her friends, including Marine Gunnery Sergeant Pam Moore. Pam was a single mom stationed at Camp Pendleton. She and Kari had become fast friends, as Pam was a Marine just like Kyle, and she and Kari had had babies around the same time.

I was very comfortable with Pam and developed a genuine friendship with her. I could call and talk to Pam on the phone and Pam would often come by to visit me.

In 1999, Kari married Kyle. Shortly after their wedding, Kari came home with the news that Kyle's Marine unit was transferring to North Carolina. I felt I simply could not follow them to the other side of the country. I would leave behind so many family members including Paul and his wife, who were within a reasonable driving distance if I found someone to drive me.

Despite the fact that Kari and I had fought frequently when we lived together, I now yearned to talk with her now that we lived so far apart. Ironically, almost the second we parted, we each incurred hundred-dollar phone bills so that we could keep constantly in touch.

Like the proverbial knight on a white horse, Pam saved the day by telling me I could come live with her and her three sons.

I appreciated Pam's kind offer, but felt I must warn her that having me come to live with them would not be easy. I emphasized what an obligation this would be on Pam's part; even though I would try my best not to call on her except out of genuine necessity, caring for me would be a huge responsibility nonetheless. Medicare/MediCal provided a bath aide to tend to me daily, and a nurse as well as an aide to do my laundry and wash my linens. But still they couldn't be with me all the time so the burden would fall on Pam.

Pam enthusiastically waved all that aside, telling me I could move in as soon as I wanted.

"I want you to come live with us, I really do," Pam assured me.

I knew all too well the full enormity of the decision Pam had made. I also recognized that no matter how generous and good-hearted Pam was, I would still be an outsider coming into their family setting. I was well aware of the challenges that lay ahead for both Pam and I. Even so, I decided to take Pam up on her offer.

Later that year Pam was assigned on-base housing at Camp Pendleton.

The on-base house was nearly brand new and Pam was breathless with excitement about it. She described in great detail the two-story, four-bedroom home with a den, family room, dining room, and covered patio. The cherry on top was the fact that the ocean was visible from some of the rooms!

"I can't believe it!" Pam exclaimed. "I'll let you have the room of your choice. There are rooms on both the upper and lower levels with a view of the Pacific. You're going to love it!" she promised me.

The reality didn't quite live up to expectations, as far as I was concerned. I was erroneously expecting a beachfront home. Granted you could see the water from the patio, the living room windows, and the downstairs master bedroom, but a romantic view it was not. The beach was located about a mile and a half away on the opposite side of Highway I-5, eight lanes of congested traffic that ran along the coast.

But, Pam was delighted with the home and I was happy for her. Eventually I trained myself to overlook the clogged lanes of traffic on I-5 and focus instead on the Pacific Ocean.

I selected the downstairs master bedroom with its own bath. I knew this arrangement would be convenient for my caretaker aide. From the living room there was a short hallway that led to the second floor stairs; my room was down this hallway on the left, with the laundry / garage on the right. The laundry room had storage and another door opened directly to the garage.

I don't know how those new doors, like the ones to the laundry room and garage were made, but they had to be slammed in order to shut properly. Ever since the shooting, my reaction to loud sounds has been dramatic. Instead of a normal reaction such as a wince or a tingling, my entire back jerked with spasms. It felt like someone was hitting me in the back with a paddle that had sharp nails sticking out of it. Every time someone slammed a door, I suffered an involuntary response that was less than pleasant. Since the doors had to be slammed shut, a reasonable solution eluded me.

On the plus side, the move to base housing reduced our expenses because housing was cheaper. Both Pam and I could now afford a few other things that we couldn't swing before.

CHAPTER 25

Helping a Friend

I was living with Pam when I received a disturbing phone call. I learned that one of Paul's high school friends, twenty-five-year-old Nicole, had been struck by a van and was paralyzed in both legs in much the same way as me.

I remembered Nicole vividly and with great fondness. Nicole had been part of the crowd of teens that hung out at my house in Scotts Mills. Mysteriously and inexplicably, Nicole and I had always had a special bond, despite our age difference.

I reeled at the terrible news about Nicole. Nicole had been standing on a street corner, waiting to cross, when a van came up over the sidewalk. She was hit and dragged under the van for a thousand feet. Her right foot was cut off and she was paralyzed.

At the time of the accident, Nicole was a single mother with a seven-year-old son. I immediately got in contact with Nicole to offer her compassion, concern, and love.

Despite our geographic separation, Nicole and I resumed our close connection as she went about the staggering process of learning what it's like to be a paraplegic. I was relieved and delighted that I could be a source of help and comfort to Nicole. I had been going through an intense depression, but once I reached out to help Nicole, my depression dissolved.

God does things for a reason, and He put us back together again to help each other.

Because Nicole was spending so much time in hospital settings, I wanted to be certain she was aware that hospitals are obligated to treat patients with respect and dignity. I explained to Nicole that sometimes the technicians doing the testing procedures are not particularly concerned with a patient's modesty. I advised her to insist on proper treatment, but also to be realistic. When having an x-ray done, for example, sometimes the technicians have to get patients in various positions in order to get a good picture of what is going on. I told Nicole that it's really helpful to lose some of your ego and have a higher threshold for embarrassment. It just comes with the territory. If you can let go of your modesty, within reason, you'll get along better.

During one particular conversation, Nicole admitted she was having a tough time because her parents simply would not accept her disability. Her mother would say, "Someday there will be a miracle because you deserve one."

Of course, miracles are always welcome, but the truth is, as I have pointed out, you don't know what the spiritual purpose of the accident was and whether or not a miracle is in order. Perhaps, and most likely, the person needs to adapt to life the way it is, not the way it might be if a miracle occurred.

I understood, however, what would prompt Nicole's mother to say such a thing and keep repeating it. It was only natural she would want her beloved daughter to be whole and well again. But I knew full well how those comments made Nicole's own process and adjustment harder. Plus it was not helpful to reinforce how much Nicole deserved a miracle, because if a miracle did not materialize, then the covert message implied was "I guess I didn't deserve a miracle after all." Not a good thing to say, regardless of how well intended.

After such a catastrophic injury, a person has to work hard with his or her new body. I didn't feel that my parents had wanted me to accept my new reality and certainly they hadn't wanted to accept it themselves. I knew it was imperative for me to learn to live with my state of being. In my mind I knew that if a miracle came along, I would have no trouble at all getting back to "normal," but in the meantime, I had to get on with my life under the current circumstances. So did Nicole.

My conversations with Nicole revealed that the attitude of Nicole's parents' was driving a wedge between them and their daughter. Nicole ended up trying to protect herself by pulling away from her parents. Her insurance paid for a double-wide mobile home where she and her son lived in the beautiful mountains of Oregon, a distance from her mother and father.

I gently and consistently gave Nicole hard-won advice about how to cope best with the state in which she now found herself.

"Well, honey, I hate to tell you, but it's going to take a couple of years to adjust. This isn't something you overcome like recovering from surgery. This is an ongoing thing and one of your challenges will be to overcome those people who just don't understand or care."

I remembered people who had treated me with a lack of understanding or lack of compassion over the years.

"They don't even know they're doing it," I said. "Even family members start treating you like a child just because you've lost the use of your legs. Often your opinion seems unwanted and unappreciated."

These encounters with people would leave me feeling down and, unfortunately they still happen to this day. Understandably I get frustrated because I hoped that when people saw me raising my family and paying my own way they would give me credit for such incredible accomplishments. Instead I felt people treated me as if I had no brains. I felt I was given little respect. I hypothesized that people think those of us in wheelchairs are children. We are only physically like children because we are short. We are always sitting down. But, our minds are grownup minds.

I revealed to Nicole that most handicapped people suffer from depression and that I had been on antidepressant drugs ever since my accident. "In fact, everyone I know who is handicapped is on them, too," I admitted. "Of course," I laughed as I attempted to soften the revelation, "Nowadays, most of the general population is on them, too. So for once, we're right in vogue!"

During one phone exchange, while we were racking up a huge long distance bill, I had to chuckle because I was so aware that Nicole was still a "kick in the pants!" Nicole revealed that she was going to see her urologist in Salem, Oregon.

"You are?" I asked. "I used to go to Dr. Carter."

"That's exactly who my doctor is," Nicole responded.

"Tell him I say 'Hello,'" I said.

And she did. The next time we spoke, Nicole said to me, "Well, I told Dr. Carter that we are buddies and he said he doesn't doubt it a bit because we both have the same attitude!"

Meaning we are stubborn!

Living Challenges

At first, everything went well living with Pam and her three boys. The boys, ages sixteen, twelve and ten, were rambunctious and mischievous, and pretty much ran roughshod over their mother. As time went on, they became more and more of a problem for Pam and me.

Pam was effusive in her affection for me, frequently hugging me and telling me how glad she was that I was with her and how much she and the boys loved me. Pam's mother added another dimension of acceptance and affection, assuring me that I was a family member now, no question about it.

"Just accept it. You are family whether you like it or not. God put you here for a reason," Pam's mother said.

Both Pam and her mother were deeply committed to Christianity and conversations often focused on aspects of their beliefs and religion. I was delighted to learn more, especially since my parents hadn't made religion a part of our lives. Although my mother always believed in God, my dad's atheism prevented mom from sharing beliefs with us except in subtle, quiet ways.

Now in this new environment, I enjoyed the chance to hear Pam and her mother talk about their beliefs and to see how meaningful Christianity was in their lives. They showed me so much about Christianity that I had never experienced before.

Pam's heart was in the right place and she had intended to take good care of me, however, as time went on things just didn't turn out that way. Pam had simply taken on more than she could handle which had near fatal consequences for me.

Because Pam was busy raising her three difficult sons and trying to keep her head above water financially, more and more things fell by the wayside where I was concerned. As the year of living with Pam's family progressed, things deteriorated rapidly and dramatically.

Although my aide tended to me faithfully, she obviously could not be with me 24/7. During the aide's absence, my care became practically nonexistent. I didn't get proper care, didn't get fed regularly, and didn't get changed. My fragile health took a nosedive until I was close to death.

One day my doctor made an emergency phone call to Kari in North Carolina.

"I know you're all the way out on the East Coast, but this is truly a case of life and death. Your mom has pneumonia and is in and out of the hospital. Without proper nutrition, regular attention, gentle care, and timely medication, she won't make it. She desperately needs proper care," he said. He told her that I was extremely sick and that unless Kari came to get me, I would not survive.

I would have let it all go until I died but the doctor sounded the alarm. I didn't have the mental clarity to pick up the phone to call Kari myself. Thank goodness the doctor did!

Kari sprang into action immediately. She called me to tell me she was flying to California and was taking me to North Carolina to live with her and Kyle. I was too foggy to fully comprehend what she was saying, but later would recognize that my daughter saved my life.

When Kyle proposed to Kari, she told Kyle that her mother goes with her! What more could I ask for?

After living only two years in California, I was moving again and I had to divest myself of still more personal possessions. My son Paul came to pack up my belongings and put them into storage. I could only take the few possessions I could carry on the plane.

I was heading to North Carolina.

CHAPTER 27

Losing My Mother

My mother had been a constant in my life and now twenty-five years after I moved away, I faced losing her. My sister Charlene gave me regular reports of our mother's state of health. We were fortunate to find a family that took in a limited number of elderly people who required the type of attention and care usually provided by nursing homes. Our mother was living in such a place not far from Charlene in Southern California. It worked out well that Charlene was close enough to visit Mom regularly.

Because of my delicate state and immobility, I didn't get many chances to visit with my mother when I lived in California. I would have loved to see Mom regularly, but it got to the point where Mom could no longer travel to see me and so I was stuck with infrequent visits. Nonetheless, even though my mother was losing her mental faculties, she always recognized me and addressed me by name. Naturally this warmed my heart because I loved my mother dearly.

One day in 2001, my sister Charlene called. Kim answered the phone and Charlene gave her the distressing news. Kim called Kari and they discussed the best way to tell me, but in the end, they decided there was no good way to break the news to me that my mother had died. When I was told, I nearly collapsed.

The stress precipitated an immediate and even more severe health crisis for me. My stomach had already been giving me fits and now it went into hyper drive, resulting in a massive bleeding ulcer.

No matter how much I wanted to fly to California for the funeral, it was utterly impossible due to my physical state, so the kids went. I waved goodbye to Kari as she left for California. Paul was already in California. Kim would fly in from Oregon. Kevin was indisposed in prison, and could not go.

My mother's death was much harder to absorb than my dad's death. I simply couldn't bear the thought of not having my mother on earth to be there for me like she'd always been.

I was devastated.

Wayne and I maintained a friendship by phone until I found out he had died of a heart attack. He never did help me out financially with the children except for one or two rare occasions like when he gave me money to purchase Kari's car. And he never stopped drinking. He'd had a previous heart attack, had lost weight, and had tried to get into shape, but he clung relentlessly to the bottle until the day he died.

CHAPTER 28

Reflections on Darkness and Light

Suicidal thoughts plagued me. When I was living with Pam, I'd look out the window from my bed and see the freeway and see all those people coming and going, but I couldn't join them and, anyways, I had no place to go. I was wrestling with the question: If the doctor puts you to sleep; it's not suicide, is it? But, of course, I never mentioned my thoughts to any of my doctors. I did talk to the children about it, however.

This was at a time when I had totally lost hope. I used to be such a people person, always going out and having fun.

During my physical decline, my mental faculties suffered as well. I simply wasn't in my right mind.

When you're lying in bed, you no longer have anything to talk about but yourself because that's your whole focus. I just didn't want to be that kind of person, but since I had a lot of time on my hands, I reflected on what people thought about me and what I thought about myself.

I am not bitter, nor am I accusatory. I never once blamed Ron, even though that would have been a convenient and handy place to land. But it was crystal clear to me from the beginning that the accident was absolutely not Ron's fault. No one was at fault, in my mind.

People see me as being very strong-willed and strong emotionally as well. They think I am strong enough to stay in bed for five years and still have some get-up-and-go left, but I don't have much of that left to go around. My back is killing me; my stomach, shoulders and arms are killing me. And my shoulder problems have really ruined my life, not the shooting per se, but what happened afterward.

And I also thought about religion because positive things always happen when I'm down at my lowest point, so I really know He's hearing me.

I've always believed that Jesus died for me. I've always believed in God even when I was a little girl with absolutely no church background to direct me. I just knew that He was always there.

As I've said, my dad was an avowed atheist and my mother was a quiet believer, I wasn't reared in a religiously oriented household. My father only gave the possibility of God's existence a teeny window of opportunity after I was shot. But that didn't keep me from believing and searching on my own.

I avoided the trap of following my father's beliefs. Being an atheist, his take would have been: If God didn't heal you and return you to wholeness then God didn't exist. I feel like the wisdom of my soul is evident as it would have been easy to capitulate to such a position, but I was never even mildly tempted.

The most intense church-going event was my baptism in a frigid Oregon river. My baptism really meant a great deal to me. I felt lighter and had a more direct connection with God after that. It was as if my baptism put me on a higher path than before.

My view is the big picture, the really BIG picture. I know there is a purpose to all I have gone through, although I haven't got a clue what that purpose might be. But I have faith and trust in God and His purpose for me.

I feel very strongly that it's a totally personal relationship between a person and their god. I don't need to know where anyone is with the Lord; it's not my business.

I won't stop being friends with someone based on whether they attend church or not. To me, the crux of the matter is whether you're a good person or not, living a good life.

If you're a good person, He's going to grab you sooner or later. That's for His time, not mine. Heaven knows the dark nights of my soul. My whole life has consisted of surges of ups and down, punctuated by a lot of downs, in fact. Whenever there's a little "up," it seems like there is a great big "down" right around the corner.

I really don't doubt that God is there for me. I desire to turn it over to Him and just put it all in his Hands and let Him take care of it. My job is to pray and turn it over. The rest is up to God, I know.

I still grapple with the question of "Why." Why has God kept me alive for so long? Why have I had such difficult challenges for most of my life?

I confess that I'm confused sometimes. Is God looking at us as a whole group of people or looking at each of us personally? Sometimes I feel so close to Him personally that I can talk to Him and hear or feel answers from Him. Then there are other times when I don't have those feelings because it doesn't seem like my prayers are being answered; nothing is getting better despite my prayers.

I've often been lonely, afraid, in pain, depressed, and sometimes bored. I've been in and out of depression, but eventually I come out of it. I store things in the back of my brain that I can't really handle and I leave them there. I'll get the really big picture once I make my transition. I'm ready for the other side.

I wouldn't be sad if I died. Then I'd be out of pain. It's supposed to be beautiful, wonderful, and peaceful on the other side.

CHAPTER 29

Giving Up Smoking

My medical problems still persisted. I had to stay in the hospital with pneumonia for several months and was forced to wear oxygen 24/7. Even after I returned home I had to stay on oxygen. Fortunately the oxygen unit had a forty foot cord, enabling me to enjoy some latitude of movement.

I stopped smoking cigarettes during this stay at the hospital. The bad news/good news is that I was too sick to care about smoking or not smoking. Once I recovered and returned home, being cigarette-free was challenging. Nevertheless, I was determined to remain a nonsmoker.

Everything seemed to trigger a desire to light up; I would lie in bed wondering how I was going to occupy my time without smoking. The phone ringing and visitors would trigger a desire to smoke.

Doctors gave me a prescription drug which I had to take for a full week before it took effect. Eventually it got into my system and created a genuine dislike for the taste of cigarettes. The pills nauseated me and caused stomach aches, but I persevered.

I bolstered my resolve by remembering how times had changed and how judgmental people were about smokers and cigarette smoke. I now felt like an oddball when I smoked and people made me feel like a nasty old person. Years ago, smoking was considered cool. Today people look at you with disgust and demand righteously, "Put that thing out!"

I took pride in the fact that, even though I had smoked for forty years, my house never smelled like cigarettes because I was very particular where I smoked. I never smoked in my bedroom or bathroom. Basically, I only smoked in the evening when I was relaxing and watching television after the kids went to bed.

When I went out drinking, I would always pair a drink with a cigarette—a common habit for many. Even so, I never smoked to excess, whether drinking or not drinking.

But finally I reached the point in my life when I really and truly wanted to be free of the addiction. I was content when I had a pack of cigarettes and panicked when I was down to my final two cigarettes. For most of my adult life I did not have the luxury of being able to run out to buy a pack of cigarettes. Mostly I had to rely on others to do that for me.

Running out of cigarettes and not being able to replace them was just another reminder to me of the control I had lost over my life. I no longer wanted to experience the panic of running low on smokes and of being a social pariah. So I quit and beat that addiction.

I also gave up my fantasies of walking again.

In my dreams I am always walking, never in a wheelchair. It was disappointing to wake up and face the reality of my continued paralysis.

And after years in the wheelchair, my ability to sit upright became compromised.

CHAPTER 30

Life's Regrets

With the birth of Tiffany's son, Jackson, I became a great grandmother. Jackson is now a little over a year old. Babies were always my favorite and Jackson is no exception.

If I have any regrets, it is that I could have been a better mother. Like most mothers, I didn't really think about whether I was being a good mom. But I fear I neglected my kids in many ways and wish I had spent more time with them playing games—just being with them.

I feel like I mistreated Kim by putting more responsibility on her shoulders than she should have had to bear. And, in my view, all the kids had to take care of me after I was shot.

If I could have done better, I would have done better. I understand that I easily could have wallowed in self-pity and become bitter, mean, blaming, unforgiving, and angry. I feel I made the conscious choice to be positive, upbeat, nice, funny, and kind in the face of my challenges.

I still experience despair after all these years, but I just wait until the despair fades away and I have a good day again. Eventually, the tide turns.

Kim, Kari, and Kevin always felt Paul got favored treatment, but I say, if that's true, it was because Paul was the baby of the family. No one resents Paul or his relationship with me. The girls were old enough when Paul was born to pitch in and help take care of him, so in a way they all babied him and doted on him.

I regret that I was still married to Wayne when Paul was born and not married to his biological father. To me it meant that Paul had been born out of wedlock, although technically it wasn't true. Ron and I didn't legally marry until little Paul was five. Paul was a much-loved child and a very good child. He developed into a wonderful human being. We all love him.

Yet, it wasn't a healthy situation, but Paul was like my gift from God. Emotionally I felt like he was all mine and

I didn't have to share him with anybody. I was so proud of him for the way he was and the way he still is today. From the beginning, I've had a uniquely close and emotional relationship with Paul. I point to the fact that we like the same things with hot, fast cars at the top of the list.

I regret that Paul didn't have a relationship with his father, or even speak to Ron, for fifteen years for that matter. Finally, after many years Ron developed a strong desire to be close to Paul and admitted he had regrets about not spending much time with any of his children.

Paul harbored no ill will against his father and I said that if he chose to have a relationship with him, that would be fine.

"I want what makes you happy, Mom," Paul confirmed.

They finally reached a sort of semi-reconciliation.

Paul was willing to share his kids with their grandfather and from my perspective, this was very important since Paul and Ron went so many years without contact.

I was delighted that Paul now had a good relationship with Ron and with Ron's children from his first wife Beverly, especially their youngest boy, Mickey.

Mickey and Paul became very close and Paul often said how much he wanted to be a dad like Mickey because

Paul had watched him be so wonderful with his own two little boys. Now Paul and Mickey share the experience of fatherhood, take their kids out together, and were daddies together. I was tickled at the thought.

CHAPTER 31

Ron Is Still Alive

We have moved again due to Kyle's employment, this time from North Carolina to New Jersey. It was Christmas time and my thoughts turned to Ron.

The last time I talked with him was six or seven years ago when I told him never to call me again. He had been drinking and I had hung up on him. I was so angry with Ron as he had brought up my affair during that call and obviously was still in self-destruct mode.

Now, I couldn't help but wonder how he was and, frankly, to know if he was even alive. I doubted he was alive if he was still drinking because alcohol had nearly killed him a number of times.

On an impulse, I picked up the phone to see if he was still in Utah. I had no way of knowing whether or not he had died or had moved during the past seven years. He had taken me at my word and had not tried to contact me since I told him not to.

I was pleasantly surprised when Ron answered the phone and that he sounded sober. He was obviously delighted to hear from me and he happily informed me that he had stopped drinking entirely. This news made me happy, of course, but I was still leery. He had promised this before, after all.

This single phone call to Ron to wish him Merry Christmas and to touch base with him initiated a series of phone calls between us. In fact, he began calling me every other day. By February he insisted that he and I should get together. In fact, he told me he wanted to get back together with me and live with me.

Hope and excitement began to bubble up within me—feelings I didn't think I'd ever experience again. I had thought my life was over, but here was the love of my life saying he wanted to be with me and live with me. I held my breath; was he truly sober? Did he truly still love me? Would he accept me, colostomy bag and all?

If it had been up to Ron, we would have skipped over the "getting to know you all over again" phase, and moved in together. But I was not so eager. We decided to meet.

I had mixed feelings and felt strongly that I needed an extended visit with him to know how I really felt about him before making definitive plans. Nonetheless, the anticipation of seeing Ron again was delicious. I hoped for the best, but recognized that seeing him could be a big disappointment if he showed any signs of drinking. I remembered when I first met him and had fallen in love with him and the phenomenal, muscular physique he sported.

When Ron walked through the door I was stunned. He looked just like a little old man.

I perused his fat belly and the lost muscle tone in his arms and chest. His sixty-one years hung heavily on him, undoubtedly from the decades of alcohol abuse. I reminded myself that alcohol takes a visible toll on the body. Our relationship had been founded on such a powerful physical attraction and an off-the-charts sex life! To have him come back as a little old man was such a shock to me. It was like, well, there goes the lust!

I had to chuckle to myself while looking at this "old man," because I imagined he was thinking the same thing about me. I was no longer the petite redhead who people nicknamed Ann-Margret. In my case, my physical travails had extracted their toll and I looked older than my sixty-one years as well. We were two of a kind, and I had to laugh.

The lust may have disappeared, but the love didn't.

It wasn't long before those feelings of love for him came back to me. Being with Ron now was like slipping into a comfortable old robe: it wrapped around me and made me feel comfy, peaceful, and most importantly, loved.

There were no signs of Ron's drinking. Kyle even offered him a beer or a glass of wine and he said "no way." Apparently Ron's reconstructed esophagus had exploded from his boozing days and he was quite emphatic that he couldn't drink or he'd get deathly sick and undoubtedly die. It took a lot of years, but he finally came to the place where he was no longer willing to put his life on the line for a drink. I breathed a sigh of relief.

Ron stayed for five days before returning home to Utah. But he called me continually once we were separated. Every time he called he told me how much he missed me and how much he loved me. Soon he flew back for a ten-day visit, and after that he came back for an entire month.

It didn't take long until our relationship resumed an easy flow. It was almost as if we had never been apart. The level of comfort we felt with each other was apparent whether we were watching television or playing dominoes. Together we enjoyed baseball and football games on television and Ron was eager to take me shopping. Everything fell into place and all my nervousness and being "on guard" evaporated.

I was amazed by his continuous attention to me, regardless of the length of his visit. He waited on me hand and foot and showered me with words of love! He was so good for me; he told me he loved me all the time!

From the first time we were reunited, Ron told me how terrible he felt about running out on me after I left rehab. He insisted he wanted to make up for it now.

After spending all that time together, it was clear to me that Ron had changed in a number of positive ways. He used to be somewhat of a cold-hearted person. If an old person would come to the door, he'd shoo that person away as soon as he could, but not anymore. Ron told me about something that had happened to him in Utah.

According to Ron, bright and early one morning, an elderly lady came to his door. She said she wanted to buy one of the condos in the building and hoped to check out what her future neighbors might be like. Ron introduced himself.

During the exchange, the woman began to shake and cry. Ron invited her to sit down but that didn't quell her sobs and shakes. Ron reached over and took her hand and tried to calm her down as much as he could. He admitted he was at a loss for what to say to her.

Finally her story spilled out. She explained that her husband was in the hospital. He'd suffered a stroke, but they wouldn't let her in to see him and she simply did not know what to do. She was beside herself and wanted so much to be at her husband's side.

Once her emotional dam had burst, she told Ron her entire life history.

In the past, Ron said, he would have cut her off, but he didn't. He just sat there and held her hand while she talked with him.

I bet he felt good and had a good feeling inside after listening to her. I think that doing good things like that means you are preparing for the other side after you die. Ron admitted that he thought so too. I could tell that he had changed and for the better.

It turned out that Ron had read up on the "other side" and read books about life after death all the time. During his visits, he shared some of his favorite books on the subject with me. I think he really believed every word he's read. Our conversations were very spiritually oriented.

I believe in reincarnation. Not coming back makes no sense. After all, nature recycles, why wouldn't we? It would be very depressing to believe otherwise.

Ron and I planned on getting our own place near enough to Kari so that she could keep an eye on my health. Kari and Kyle invited Ron to live with us—if that would work out better—which is testimony to how much Ron has changed.

Kari used to hate Ron's guts but now she really likes him. We're all heartened by the fact that Ron has been to see Paul and his children. The relationship was re-emerging as well. All of this seems to confirm that the changes in Ron were impressive and for the better.

I loved the fact that Ron accepted me the way I was. It felt wonderful! Here I was paralyzed and he accepted me that way without reservation. I even changed my colostomy bag right in front of him and it didn't faze him whatsoever.

Having Ron back in my life gave me more joy and happiness. I know how sorry he was, and really, he didn't have to say it. The way he treated me told me he was sorry. It's hard to take care of me and God knows how my daughter has done it all these years.

Ron helped with my care. He loved to get me out of the house and I adored that too. I feel loved by him, in his way of loving. He kissed me a lot and he would visit me when I was in bed, taking my hand, kissing me, and telling me he loved me. It felt so good! I never thought I'd have that again. Ever!

Ron's coming back helped me mentally and emotionally. I felt wanted again. Before that I had just wanted to die because everyone had their own lives to live and nobody wanted to take care of a sixty-one-year-old paraplegic. Now I had someone who wanted to do that out of love for me, and that felt so good. Ron being back in my life was a huge blessing.

Kari and Kyle moved again and we all went to North Carolina for a while. Ron even visited me there. Then we were on the move again, this time back to California.

Ron and I finally moved into an apartment in Fallbrook, California, just like we had talked about.

CHAPTER 32

Physical scars

It was wonderful to be back with my husband and so in love again. It was a challenge for Ron to take care of me in my condition but he didn't complain. He was loving, and what more could I want?

My condition includes scars all over my chest, neck, and inner arms from what they call pencil or port lines. They were implanted in my veins in order to get various medications and fluids into my body over the years. My arm veins have become so weak that they collapse after only five to ten minutes of receiving antibiotics. Nowadays, my veins are bypassed by a central port line in my chest.

Straight lines, or central lines, require that a nurse check on me at home every twelve hours to make certain the settings are accurate, as well as to refill the medications or fluids, and clean the area where the straight line is inserted.

The list of physical problems I have endured over the years is endless. Some of the most difficult times have been precipitated by recurrent kidney and bladder problems. When my kidneys are affected, my emotions are disrupted and I get mad easily, and I cry at the drop of a hat. I can't explain it, but only know it to be true. Several times during a kidney or bladder crisis, friends have asked me if I was going crazy. Of course I'm going crazy.

Something I've never, ever gotten used to is my catheter coming out accidentally and leaking onto my bed. It brings me to tears.

What I wanted was to be free of medical complications, but I found myself back to the doctors in more pain. I convinced one of my doctors to prescribe morphine to kill the pain. It took care of the pain but it caused me to start hallucinating. I didn't know what was going on. Kari took me back to her house to live. Ron came with me. Slowly, with Kari's care, I was weaned off the morphine.

As for Ron, I was too much work for him at his age. After six months of living together he moved back to Utah, but not for good. He was still a constant visitor and helped out when Kari needed a break. I am glad that he was back in my life. And as for me, I was now in Yucca Valley, California, in the guest house behind Kari and Kyle's house.

CHAPTER 33

I Love My Babies

If I were forced to pick my favorite thing, it probably would be babies. I love babies and always have, ever since I had my first child at sixteen.

I feel the same way about all my children and grandchildren. And I'm proud to say we're a good, loving family and not an arguing bunch of maniacs like some families. When we had reunions, they were wonderful and happy. We shed happy tears about the beautiful children, and laughed over the antics of the pets and the funny things kids do. It's all good stuff. And babies are the best part of the whole deal, as far as I am concerned.

I practically lived with my first three grandchildren when I still called Oregon home. In fact, I did live with Tiffany for the first three months of her life. I was in my glory.

Tiffany was God's gift not only to her parents, but to me as well. I loved her so much and that love really got me going.

I wanted to be more independent and act like a grandma is supposed to act. I wanted to take my grandchildren with me to all sorts of places, from the circus to Toys R Us.

I take pride in how my four children have turned out, especially in light of the challenges the entire family has suffered. My paralysis fundamentally changed the life experience of each one of them. But as I've said, the big gift my paralysis gave me was the close relationship with my children. My circumstances forced me to spend time at home with them.

As of 2008, Kari has been married to Kyle for nine years, and I have lived with them for over seven years. Kyle has a nine-year-old autistic daughter and Kari has her children from her first marriage: sons Jeff and Justin are ages twenty and sixteen respectively. Kari has her real estate license and sells real estate. She supplements her income by being a waitress. The two are very happily married.

Likewise, Kim has also been happily married to Mark for about five years, although they've been together for fourteen years. They have no children together either. Tiffany is twenty-five, Jeremy is twenty-three, and Aaron is twenty-two. Kim put herself through college and went to dental school. Kim still lives in my old house in Scotts Mills, where she is a dental assistant. She loves her job and the house dearly!

Kevin is going to school to become a substance abuse counselor and lives in Salem, Oregon. He is in love with a woman, but they're not yet married. He was diagnosed with ADD and put on Ritalin, which has made all the difference in his behavior. I am thrilled to see my son finally headed in such a positive direction. I recognize that because of Kevin's own battle with drugs and alcohol, he can become a most effective counselor.

Paul lives in Orange County, California. He and his wife Patti have been married for eleven years and have two daughters: Kindra and Lauren. They, too, are happily married. Paul is an entrepreneur who started his own window and door company; he has been in business for eight years. Now he and Ron have a relationship and everyone stays in touch.

My sister Charlene is still living in California and married to her husband, Bill. Their three children are all grown and gone from the nest and now grandchildren are enriching their lives.

I have become a great grandmother with the birth of Tiffany's son, Jackson, who is a little over a year old. Babies were always my favorite and Jackson is no exception.

Besides babies, my children and grandchildren, my top-of-the-list priority is God and my faith in God. As a child, I was spiritually curious. I eagerly sampled different churches and different religions by accompanying girl friends to their churches.

The most intense church-going event was my baptism in a frigid Oregon river in January. My baptism really meant a great deal to me. I felt lighter and had a more direct connection with God after that. It was as if I was on a higher path than before.

My view is the big picture, the really BIG picture. I know there is a purpose to all I have gone through, although I haven't got a clue what that purpose might be. But I have faith and trust.

CHAPTER 34

Final Diagnosis

Like I said, I was living in Kari's quest house, in Yucca Valley, California, that was, until a forest fire broke out close to the house.

"There's fire around and we need to evacuate. We have to move," Kari said.

Only my move wasn't with them.

Because of my requirement for constant oxygen, I was placed in a nursing home with twenty-four-hour care. It was such a pleasant change to have nursing care around the clock instead of just part time. I liked it so much that I didn't want to go home with Kari and decided I would stay. Kari agreed to it.

It was great having all the care the facility could provide. My meds always arrived on time and I didn't have to worry about Kari needing to attend to me. Everything went fine for about eight months until I went into respiratory arrest brought on by too much Ativan. I was rushed to the hospital and hooked up to life support.

At this point I didn't really care about living or dying. I had been through enough that I was ready. Luckily for me, Kari came and helped me, and after several months I had recovered and I went home with Kari.

The doctors told me that I now had permanent damage to my heart and they recommended open heart surgery. The doctors told me that without surgery, I had maybe three to six months left to live.

I talked it over with Kari and I told her that I didn't want the surgery. I've had enough of tests and surgeries.

"I'll honor your wishes Mom," Kari said.

I knew it was hard for her because she had always helped me, but she couldn't help me now. However, I was prepared for the end now that there was an end in sight.

After six months I am still alive and still in pain. I am still bed-bound, still in constant pain, and still on oxygen.

It never leaves me. Ron does come and visit and that is always grand. His love is so genuine it makes me feel free.

Christmas is always a happy time with the grandkids. This Christmas of 2008 is bringing me such joy: Kari has a new baby and I am thrilled.

On Christmas Eve I open presents with Kari, Kyle, and the kids. It is a glorious night. After opening presents Kari takes me back to the guest house—my house.

Kari gets me into bed and gets my oxygen tube set up for my breathing. My cell phone is on the night stand. Kari says goodnight and Merry Christmas, and she will see me in the morning.

Epilogue

On Christmas Day, Kari picks up her cell phone to call her mother to see if she is ready to spend the holiday with the family, but her cell phone battery is dead. She walks back to the guest house to get her mother.

Kari enters the guest house and finds her mother lying quietly in bed.

Then she notices her mom's oxygen tube is on the floor instead of on her mom.

Her mom's phone is not near the bed, and as she moves closer she notices her mom is not breathing. She check's her mom's pulse but there is no pulse.

Janice Riddle finally found her rest on Christmas Day.

In March of 2009 Ron Riddle, sixty-four, dies in his home state of Utah from liver disease. He never told the family about his health problems.

Janice leaves her four children, grandchildren, and great grandchildren.

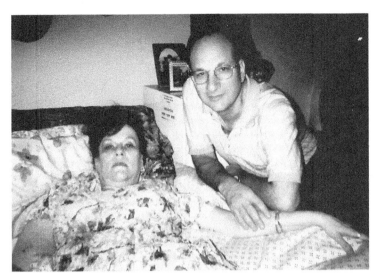

Janice Riddle and Author Richard Ballo during an interview

Other books by Richard Ballo

Life without Lisa

The Heart of Grief Relief Journal

The Unbounded Heart of Grief Relief Journal

Grief 50 Questions and Answers

360 Degrees of Grief

Martin the Mouse in the White House

Martin the Mouse in Santa's House

Martin the Mouse in a Haunted House

Martin the Mouse in a Firehouse

www.richardballo.com